AF378728

TEXT M. C. SIGRIST / LAYOUT P. WASSERMANN / LITHOS KIRSCHBAUM LASERSCAN GMBH DÜSSELDORF / FOTOSATZ UND DRUCK MEIER + CIE AG SCHAFFHAUSEN

CHRISTIAN VOGT

PHOTEDITION 5

Who is Christian Vogt? With this somewhat banal question I do not primarily mean the side which most connoisseurs of demanding photographic art know of the photographer who was born in Basle, Switzerland, in 1946. What I am looking for is the person behind those prints exhibited in galleries and not the obviously extroverted side of the artist. I would like to know how Christian Vogt thinks and works. (Whereby here, I must admit that I, by far prefer the thinking progress that precedes his works to the expressive side of his photographs.) Furthermore, I would like to know how he lives, as I consider such a question perfectly legitimate. Whenever possible, I have allowed Christian Vogt to speak for himself. Even though, one might here get the impression, that quoting word for word a man's ideas and thoughts about himself and his work may only be considered as a form of journalistic realism. This could on the surface be true, although it doesn't get to the heart of the real reason. It is therefore evident, that the such clear and defined convictions of a brilliant mind such as Christian Vogt's ("Only the real things that I experience through this medium and the working progress, do matter.") would, in an inadmissable way, be either drawn out of context or manipulated in one way or another, when channelled indirectly into the personal opinion of a third person.

Christian Vogt spent the first six years of his life with his grandmother, in a large house, situated in a vast, rund-down garden. These years of childhood in retrospect represent for him a most valuable time. More or less subconsciously, he has experienced an intensive contact with nature, with a free and untamed world of plants. Coupled with his childhood fantasy, this part of his life has remained something magical for him. Those happy, early years were, and still are the source of energy, which inspires him.

Christian Vogts present working place is in some way just as dreamlike and strange. Crammed into the center of the busiest section of Basle and surrounded by the so-called modern business-centers is a huge an spectacular villa, slightly burlesque art nouveau – with the trimmings of inner court and staircase and which due to its bulk creates a frighteningly mausoleum impression. Whoever had the idea that an undoubtedly "arrived" photographer – (Maybe you don't like the expression – but it's accurate) – would surround himself with at least adequate, if not exotic or flipped-out facilities, would be disappointed. The spacious, well lit rooms are sparsley furnished, and totally functional, but they by no means give the impression of being cold. This is a working place, something which one observes without taking into account the array of technical equipment. The surroundings are not dominant, it is the auro of the creative, omni-present spirit of its inhabitant.

Christian Vogt himself – may he not oppose to this personal description – is not only a "nice man". He is intelligent, attentive, and agile in his ways, he might sound a trifle provocative in his persuasive and convincing way, but never superficial, never thoughtless in his process of thinking. And is above all a very lovable person. "I like to be able to embrace the people I work with," he once wrote. Those who would take the trouble to meet him would experience the same feeling. In his studio, which by now is relatively well known due to its painted round horizons (to be seen in his latest book "Eighty-two photographs with fifty-five women"), Peter Wassermann and he himself carefully selected the photographs for this publication, choosing three themes to make up the whole.

Here, on one of the upper floors, he works, when he is doing "inside" work. This he does mostly in the company of his two cats and – what is far more important – in the company of his companion Susan Nash, who is his most important and only collegue – insofar as creativity is concerned and who is also his most critical viewer.

Let us return to his childhood in Grandma's wild garden. Travelling has also influenced him strongly – he loves to travel and travels a great deal –. Asia presented him the essential impulses, which have become part of the section "Onlookers" in this volume; America, he came to know and understand through the eye of the commercial photographer and through his various Polaroid-advertising photographs. The exhibition of his work here has brought him feed-back for his artistic work from yet another continent. Artistic work? What does that mean to Christian Vogt, who could probably live quite comfortably on what he earns from his own photography, but who despite this, and possibly because of it, states that he earns his daily bread chiefly from "Commercials". – He is well known and has a good name in the advertising field, something which should not be underestimated, and can therefore afford to be selective. He is not however, too choosey as far as the fee is concerned. (The amount doesn't seem important to him and may vary a lot.) Even the type of project is not as important as the "how" of the task. Freedom, which is a necessity for a creatively working person, is for him absolutely essential. Only with sufficient freedom he is capable of creating successful, co-operative work, should they be calendars for the chemical industry or advertisements for a furniture manufacturer. He finds it very regretful too – that for whatever the reasons may be, a photographer in advertisement photography today is seldom consulted or actually involved in a conception and thereby encouraged to think. Why – and Christian Vogt asks this in all earnest, do the lay-outer and copy-writer always have to come to the photographer with an almost finished conception or design, why can't they let him also contribute to the search for the idea? Basically, that is by no means being choosey. On the contrary, it confirms that Christian Vogt is almost always ready to participate in a demanding job.

Is he a commercial art photographer? His own opinion to his vast success in both fields he sums up as follows: "I don't care whether I am seen as a photographer or as an artist – I don't identify myself with anything – not with any kind of photography either –. Leth the classifiers classify – it might give them a sense of security!"

By the way, the word "art" doesn't derive from "ability" but originates from the word "announcement" (in the sense of making something known). – The three, concluded series which we have, together with Christian Vogt, chosen for this edition, only have a limited connection to eachother insofar as they carry the "trade-marks" of his own way of thinking and working. Continually impressing is how clearly and analytically he is able to think and express himself. It is a way of thinking that is distinctly reflected in the presented three series. Are his the works of an elitist? Sure, the viewer too is required to do some thinking. We'll talk about comprehension or non-comprehension later on.

"**I** don't like to talk about my work. Once I feel that I understand a series, I turn to something else and begin to look for a new form. I therefore actually stop when I've found the recipe to do a job by. (Work becomes easier and success surer.) Creative work or art for me, deals with constant renewal."

Incidently, talking about series: Christian Vogt very often chooses themes, which only throuth their frequency begin to transmit a message – their realisation however often takes years. In this connection, I like to refer to the nude-series with Romana, which he began in 1975 and which he photographs each year at just about the same time. Or his "Red Series" or of course his so-called frame-photos enter my mind. It is of the utmost importance to Christian Vogt to work on a task with patience and persistence, until that particular one is – as far as he is concerned – completed.

There are only two ways to understand Christian Vogt's photos, their message, their symbolic content. Amongst the critics and the circles who support culture ("I am hardly in touch with the relevant scene!") and among the "normal" public, are people who understand his photographs and others who don't understand them. Actually, this sweeping statement is far more complex than one may assume at first. Because:

"**T**he problem isn't that someone doesn't understand – it goes as far as that someone doesn't understand that he doesn't understand."

The two aforementioned ways of looking at this matter do of course not only mean that Christian Vogt's photographs can be either intellectually analysed or that one can be affected emotionally by them. For him as the creator, the most beautiful thing that can occur, is when he feels that the viewer accepts and understands his photos both in a rational and an emotional association. That is why I have the feeling that just the three selected photo-series – as different as they may be – can contribute a great deal to one understanding his work (and by the same token, himself) even better. Especially if – when viewing them – one thinks of his quote:

"**T**he things behind the things are the most important."

The series "Music Academy"

The photos of this series should be placed on the difficult
to define dividing line between commercial (advertising) photography and freelance artistic work. In 1975, Christian Vogt was
engaged to make a documentary on the Music Academy in
Basle. Restrictions of no kind were put on him. He divided this
documentary into the respective surroundings (there emerged
25 to 30 takes, among them the herewith presented photos)
and into portraits of musicians – interesting enough, once with
open and once with closed eyes. The Academy of Music itself
is reflected very quietly in his photos, and this in two senses.
The rooms are quiet, the doors are open. The exact reverse
of the situation during the week. When every room is alive
with music and musicians, the sounds emitted through partially
sound proofed doors. When a door opens, one can see and
hear what is behind it. Christian Vogt felt it were like an advent
calendar. The empty academy created the very same impression
and peculiar fascination, for the empty school-house during
vacation or on Sundays. When entering – also in these photographs – I could almost detect that particular smell that belongs
to school-houses and that is unique all over the world. Whoever
walks through these, due to their emptiness, slightly sinister
and by the same token solemn corridors, will only witness his
own thoughts. It was very difficult for Christian Vogt to "see"
photographs there. He first tried to capture the moods with
the 35 mm camera. It was a hopeless task. Only four years
later, when he started to use a Sinar large size camera (with
which the process became more awkward, more contemplative),
he began to feel "things behind the things". The photographer
started to perceive the photographs.

The series "Images 1982"

"**I**t is of the utmost importance to me that in the work that
I do, something comes together. – It is unimportant for me whether
the work is done outside or inside. – And not important, where
these things meld together. – It is only important, that the inner
and the outer things do get together."

"**T**he nude is only important to me because it does not have
an image. Clothes always represent something."

These reduced to "bosom and mouth" portraits (I'm afraid
that I cannot think of a better explanation) astound in view
of the really tight clippings. What a terrific "body-language"
must have taken place here, how very striking the immediate
communication between viewer and photograph. From this
very minimum, reduced as it is presented in this portrait series,
Christian Vogt was able to reach a maximum of expressiveness.
A series, which by the way, shall not be completed for a long
time yet. It will require another unlimited number of photographs
until that instant arrives when Christian Vogt will be able to
say that he is returning to a new beginning and is looking for
a new form. These portraits, no doubt, live through the compar-
ison between their different expressions and messages. It is
most remarkable as far as technique and creation are concerned
that all original prints were taken at a scale of 1:1, "Life-Size"
as Christian Vogt calls it. Gestures, or more precisely the secret
of gestures has long fascinated him: "I have been interested
in stones, feathers and gestures for a long time." Maybe it
is or was often his own body-language which he tried to apply
to somebody else (his models) until he had the feeling that
this connection had succeeded. These photographs are certainly
very profound. Just as profound as his thinking (and that doesn't
include this particular work only). Previously, without knowing
where the inspiration had come from, he drew pictures of situations which he later transmitted into photo language. He com-
ments that he knows that there is something, he believes that
he himself as a human being and artist is maybe only (or too)
an instrument of an unidentifiable outer strength. The message
of these photographs, their sign language, may not be interpreted
as surrealism.

"**W**hat kind of a world is this, where one only looks at the beautiful things, but not *behind* the ugly ones."

He admits of course, that he is again and again guided by aesthetics (which he curses here). Because he knows of the artist's satisfaction when a photo "is in tune".

As a rule, he first takes a number of Polas, to enable his models to be "there" when a photo is being created. This procedure is even more understandable when one knows how much Christian Vogt dislikes the shooting photographer on one side (of the camera) who reduces his model on the other side to a mere object. He normally examines the Polas with his models – and together they discuss and alter. I can well imagine that every time a project succeeds the resulting celebration would have that something extra in the joy of accomplishment.

"**I** am always happy when I am happy that I'm happy."

The series "Onlookers"

It is most difficult to interpret these „reversed" portraits. Christian Vogt himself makes this interpretation almost impossible by saying that there is no philosophy behind them. What fascinates us in watching someone looking at something (which doesn't remain unseen to us) is certainly not only the suspense in the structure of the picture or in the repetition of the colour used in the foreground as background. The idea for "Onlookers" originated years ago after two trips to India. Christian Vogt didn't care for the photographical output it had brought, thought the memories he had were too cliché ridden and didn't leave enough impressions to deal with. On his third trip to India, he always used a western viewer to create a contrast to the Indian reality. One, who would either gaze into the direction of the shot to be taken or at a shot that had been taken. (Two of the photographs presented in this volume bear evidence to that.) Christian Vogt discovered that the idea of viewing a viewer could easily be transferred to other circumstances and situations.

"**E**very photograph is a projection-surface."

Without wanting to idolize, the artist and perfected artisan with his precise and uncompromising photographic work, obsessed by his thinking and his creative expressiveness, reminds us of one of the master photographers who created such works of timeless beauty. It has nothing to do with wrongly understood pathos or with flattering prediction, if one nowadays claims with absolute conviction that Christian Vogt, one day too shall be one of those who will be mentioned in the history of this still new form of art; some of his work is today already considered classic in the new photography.

More appropriate than any inadequate attempt to grasp and characterise the person Christian Vogt in his universality, are the simple words of a big philosopher:

"**W**hat is called the visible equals the shape of a work of art – its value lies hidden in the invisible."   Lao Tse

Music Academy 1979

"In 1975 I was engaged to make a documentary on the Music Academy in Basle. It was however only in 1979, when I started to work with a large size camera (the process became ponderous and more contemplative) that some of the 'things behind the things' became more distinct. I divided this documentary into the surroundings (as presented here) and the portraits of musicians."

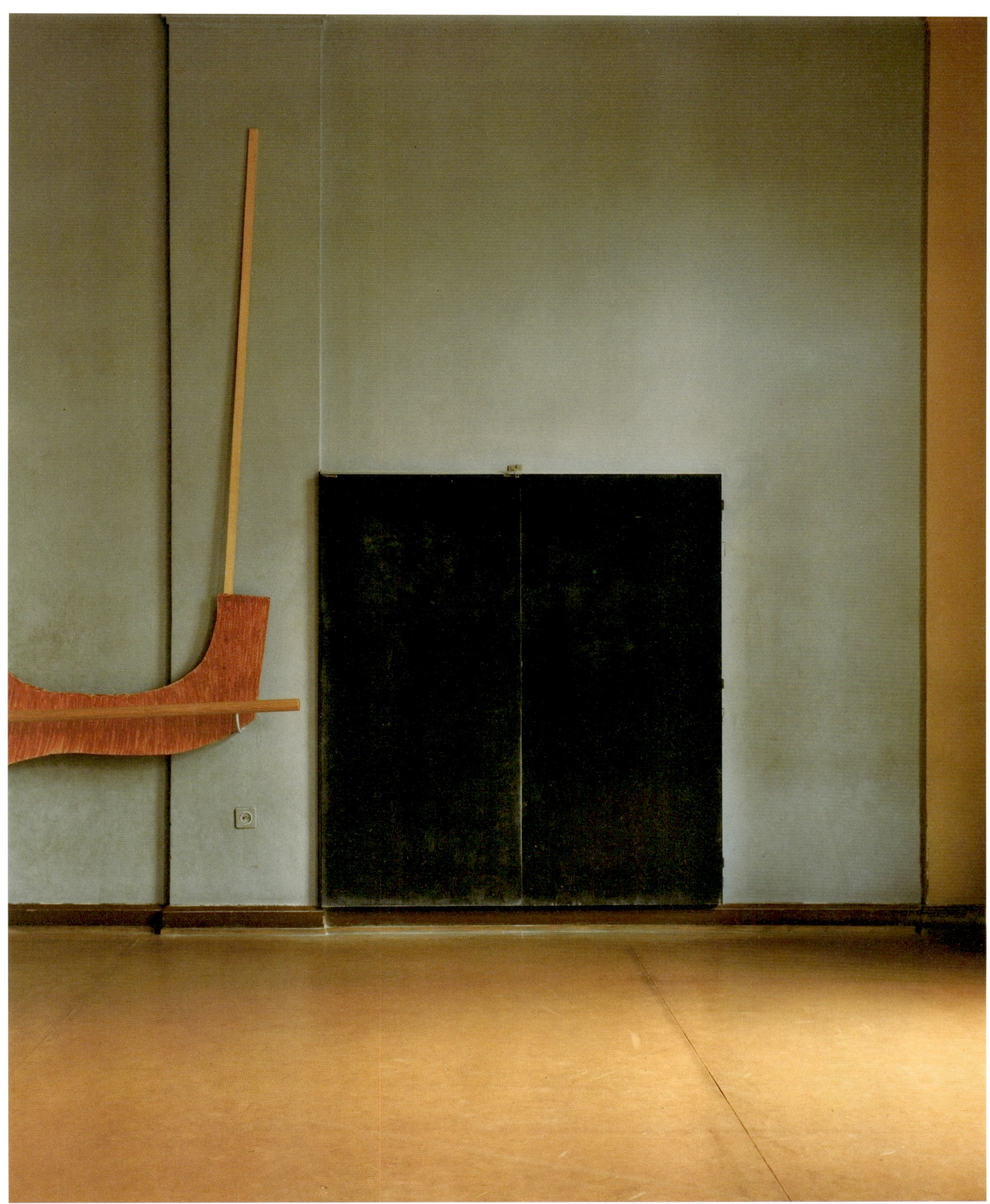

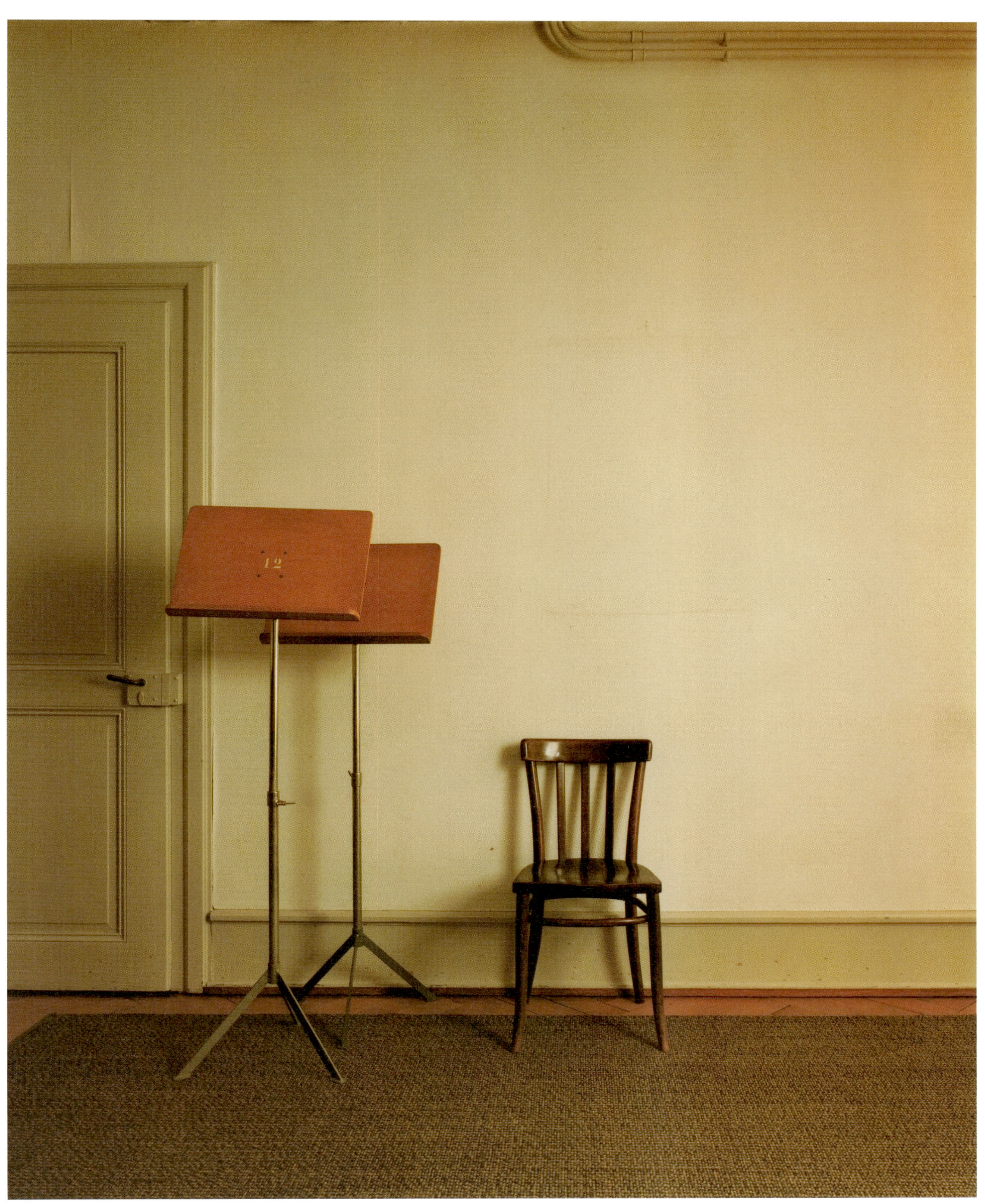
12

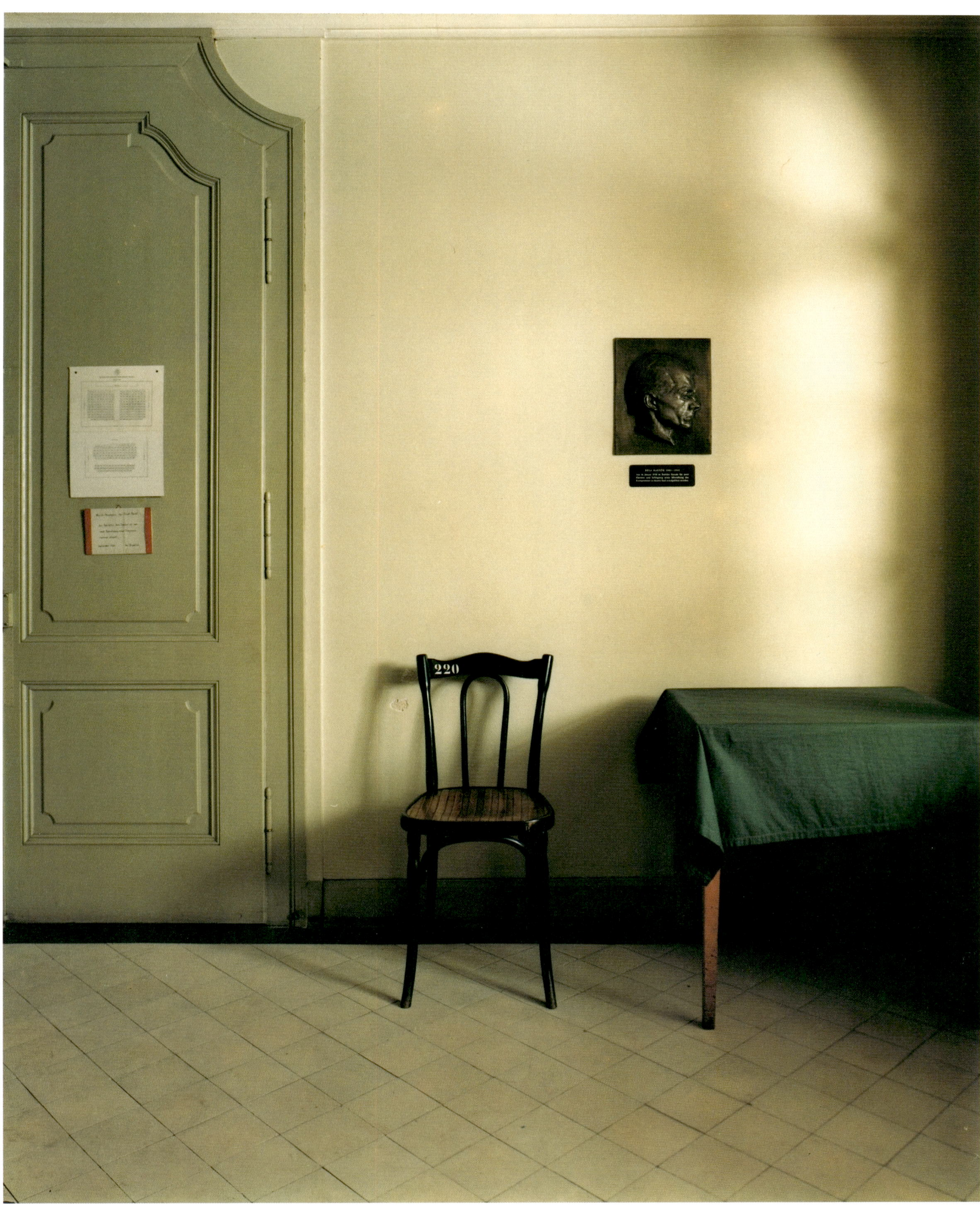

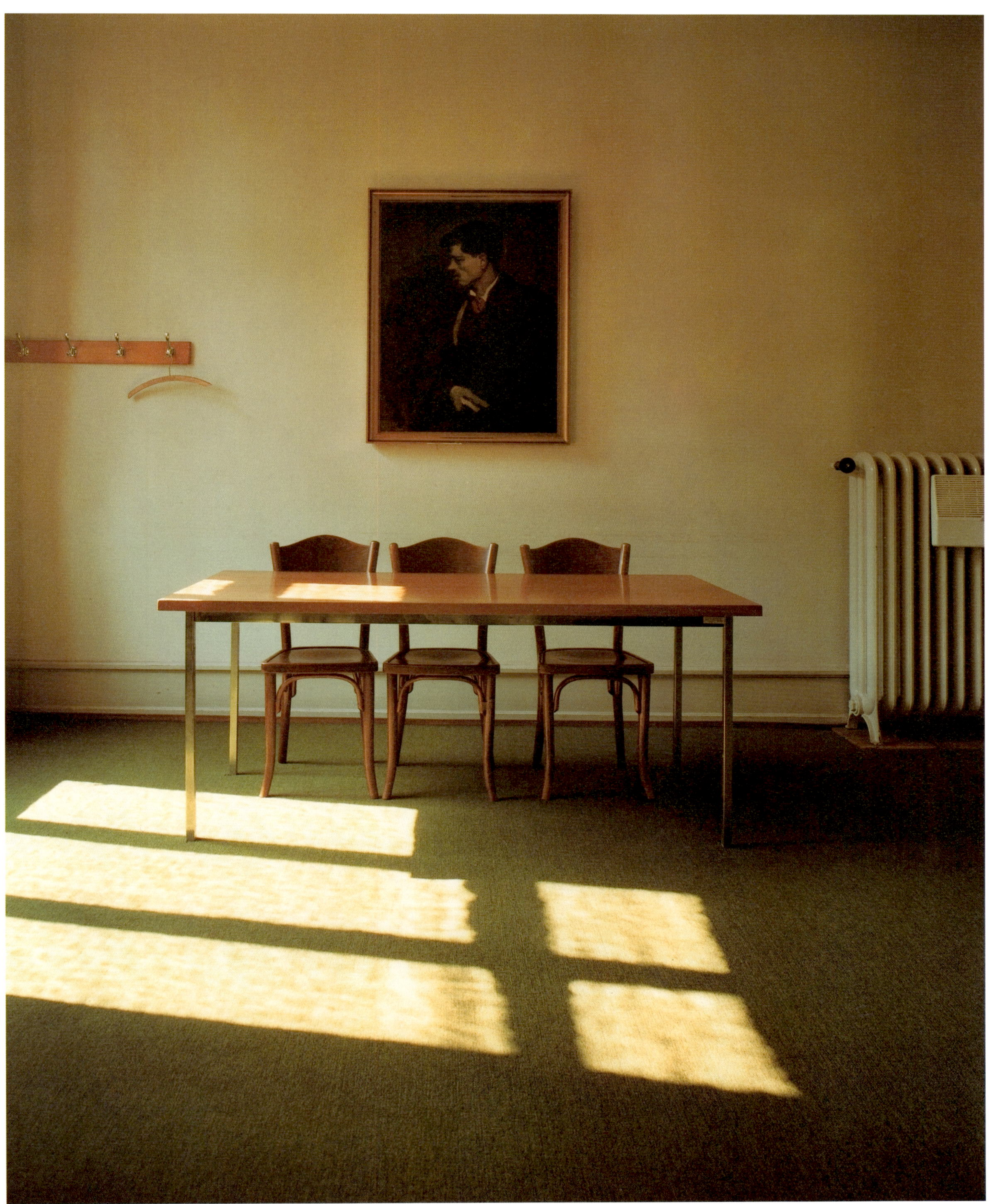

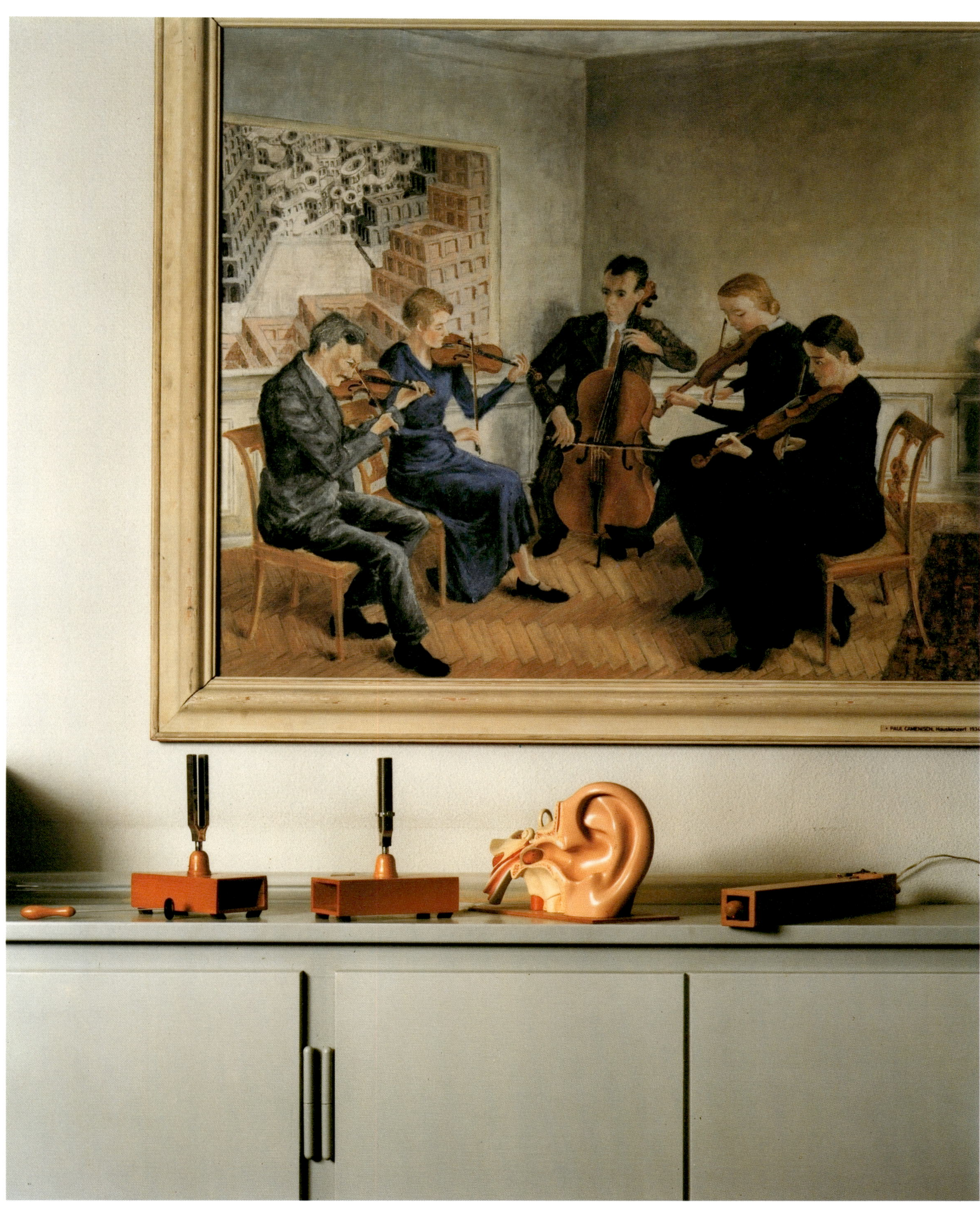
PAUL CAMENISCH, Hauskonzert 1934

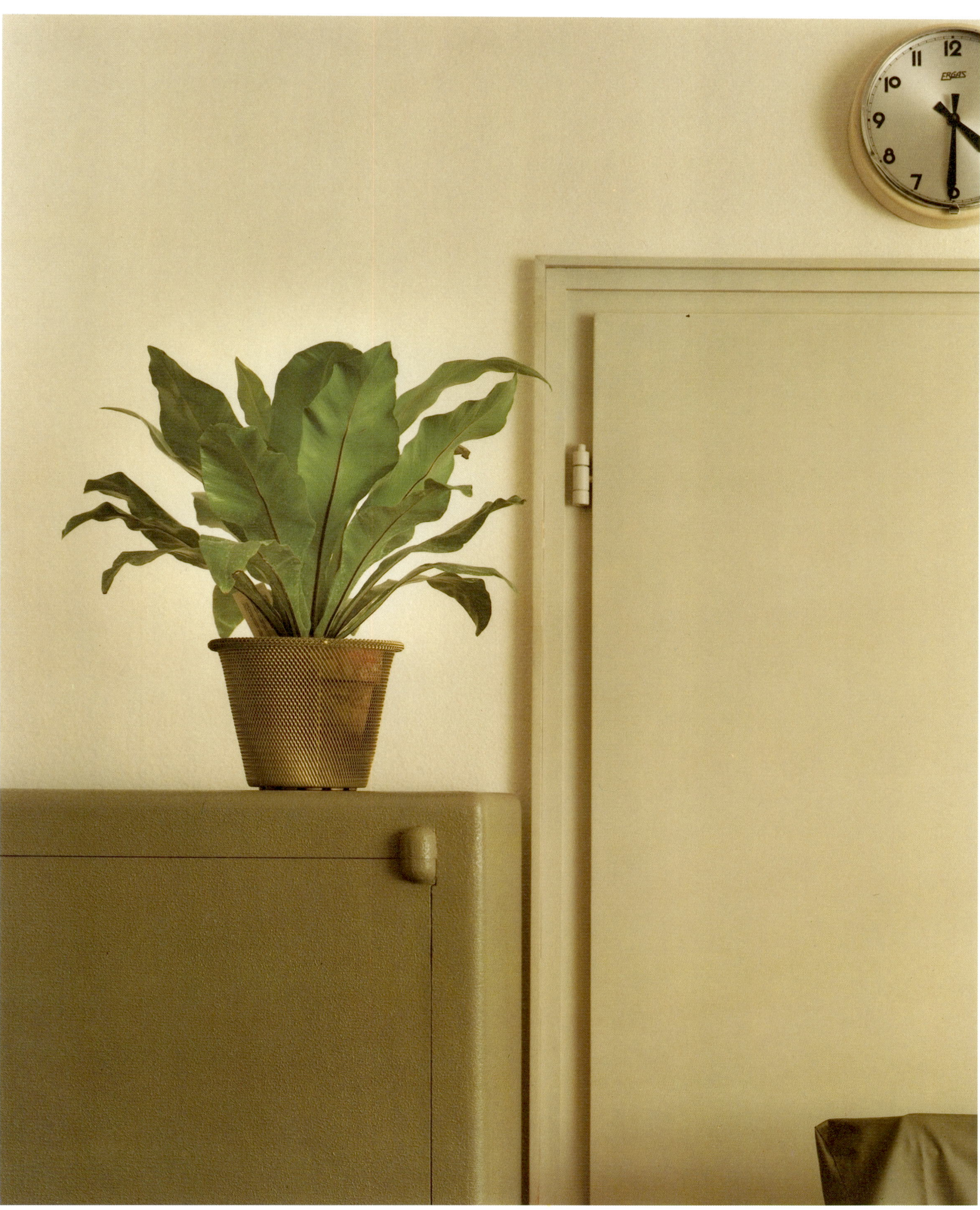

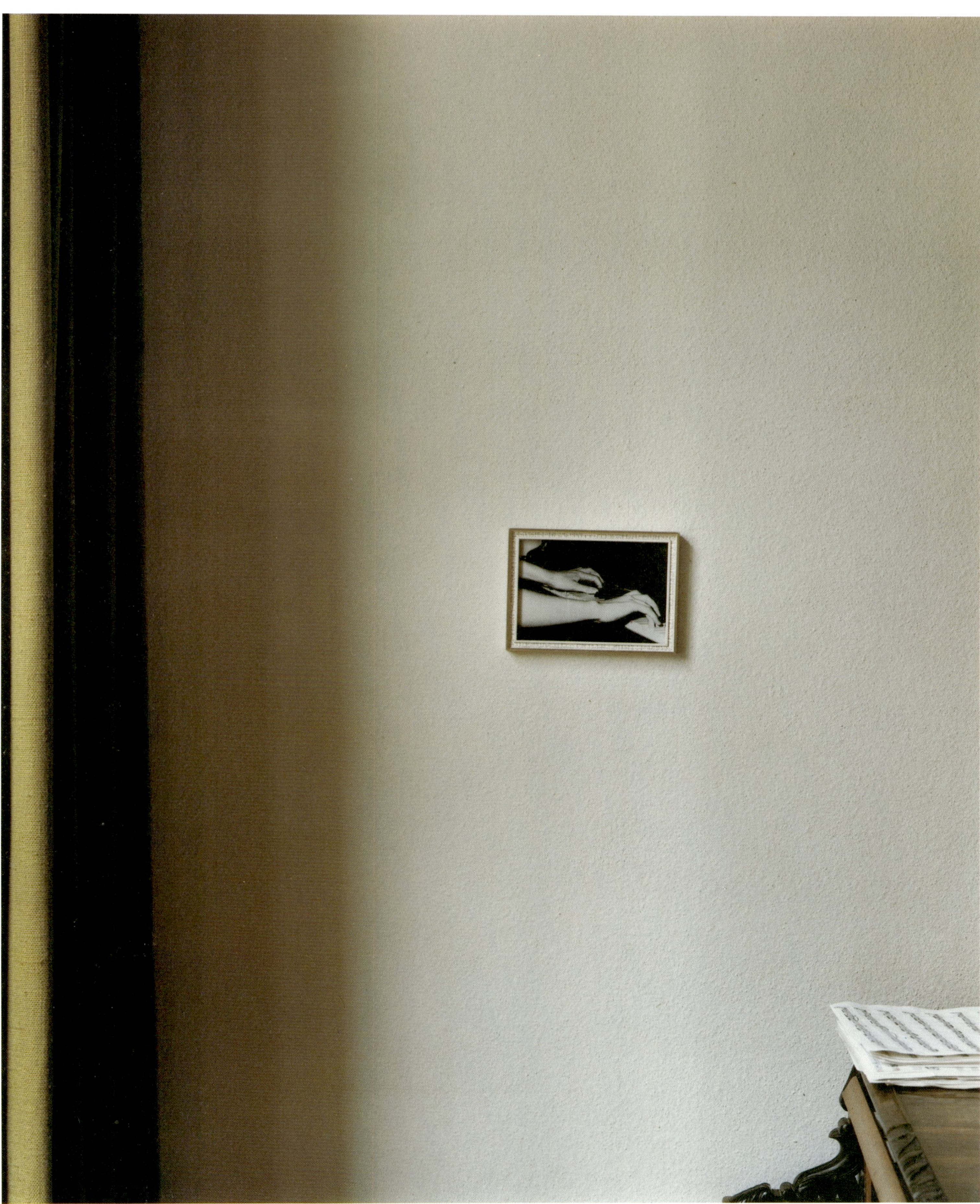

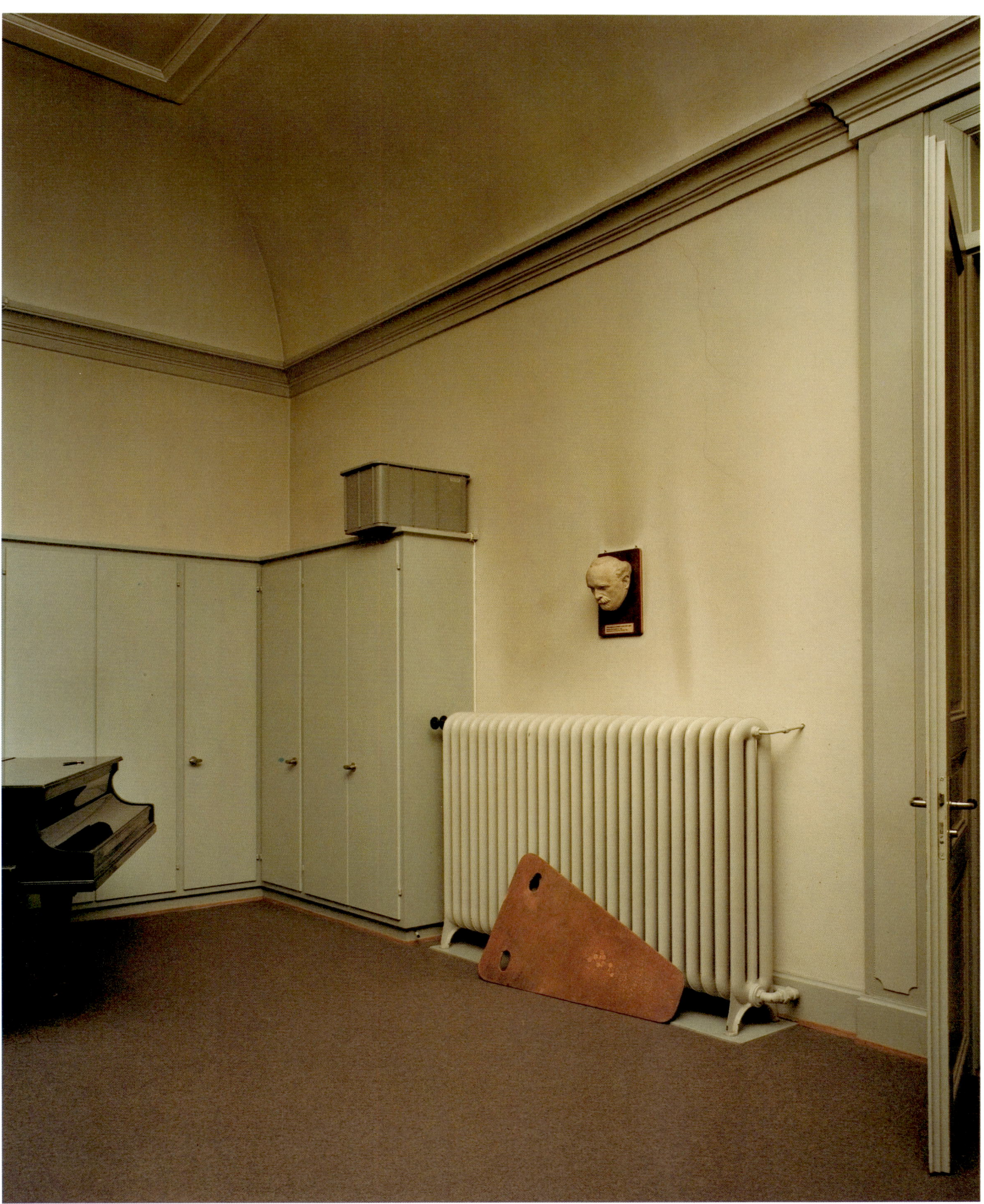

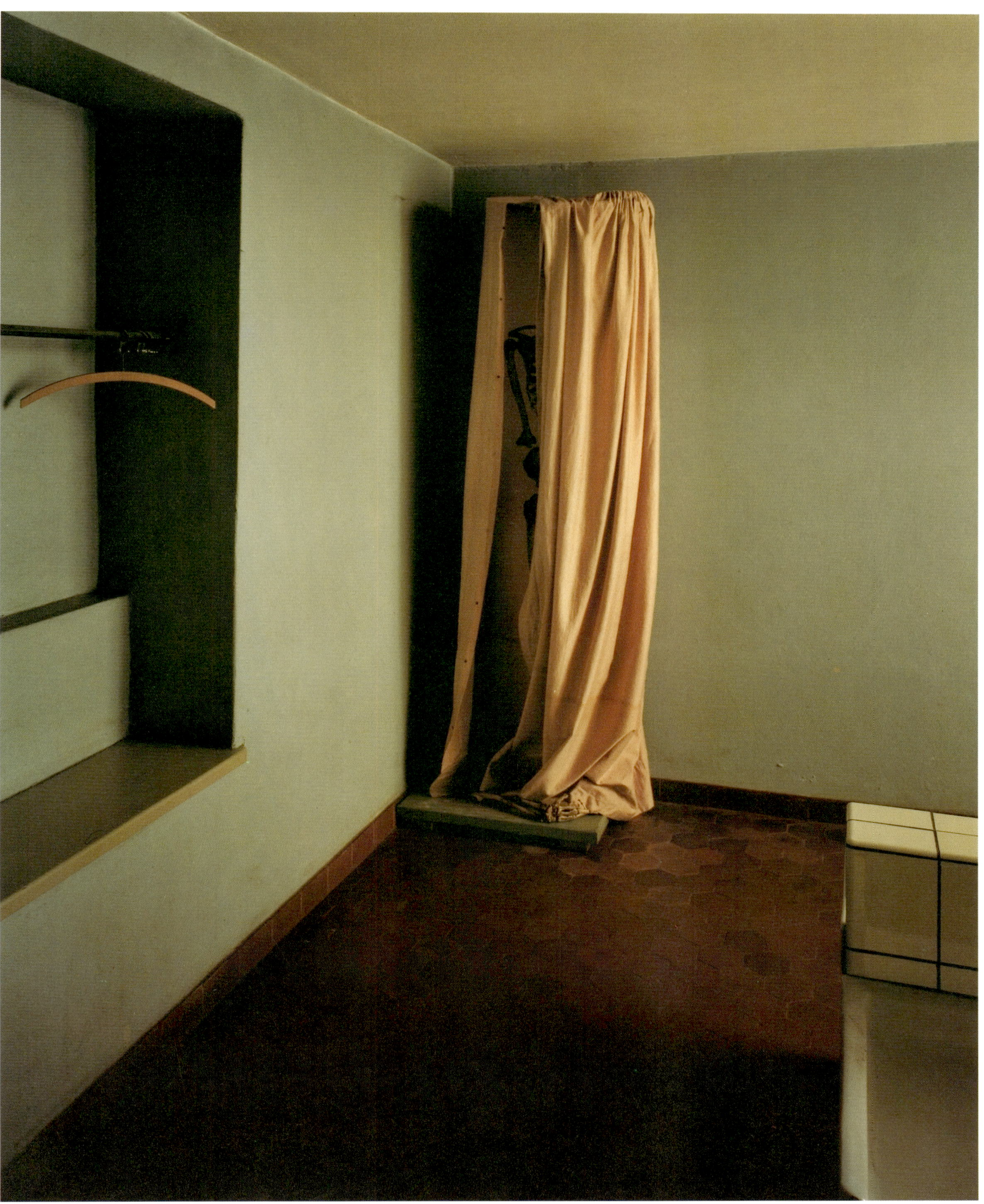

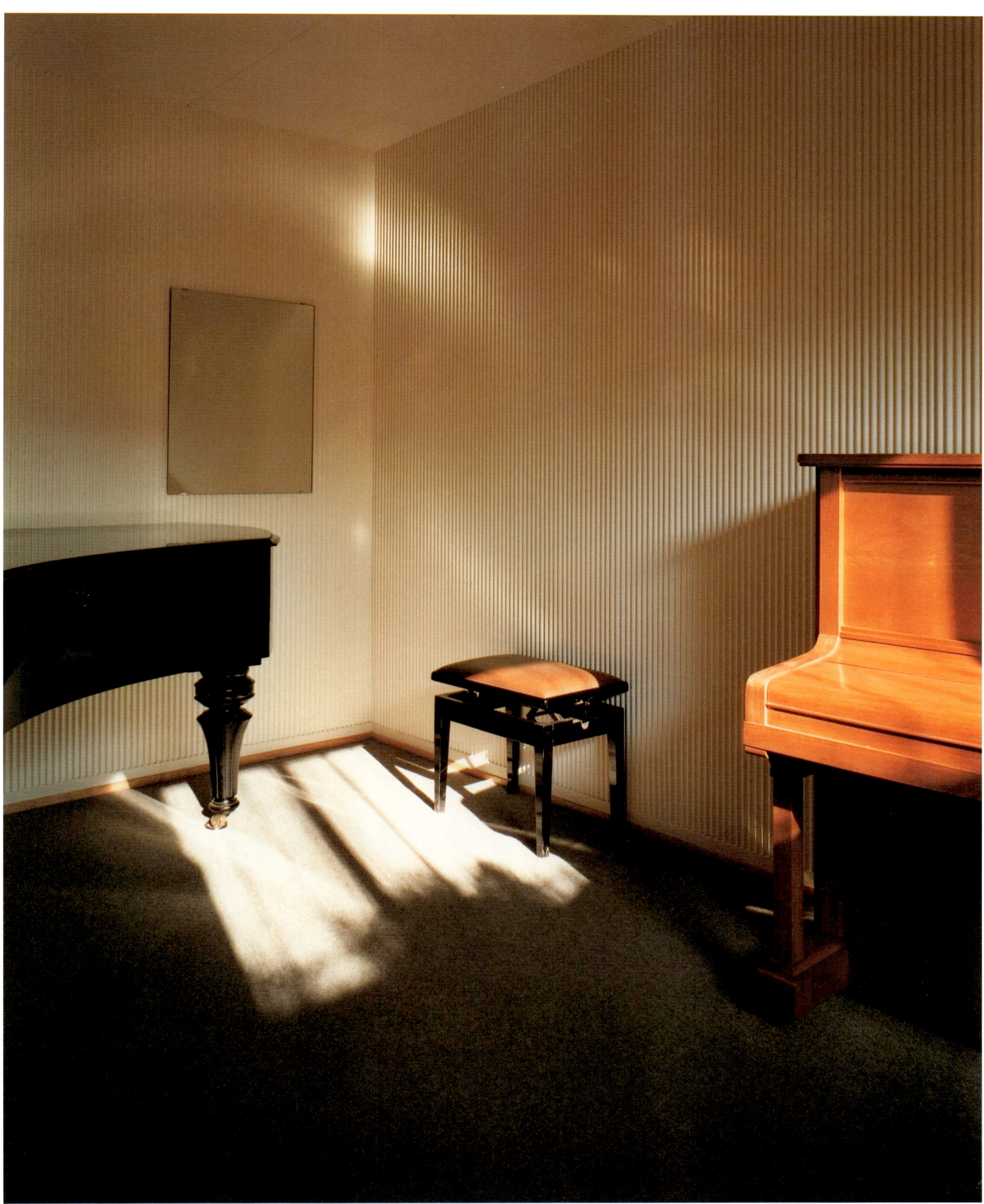

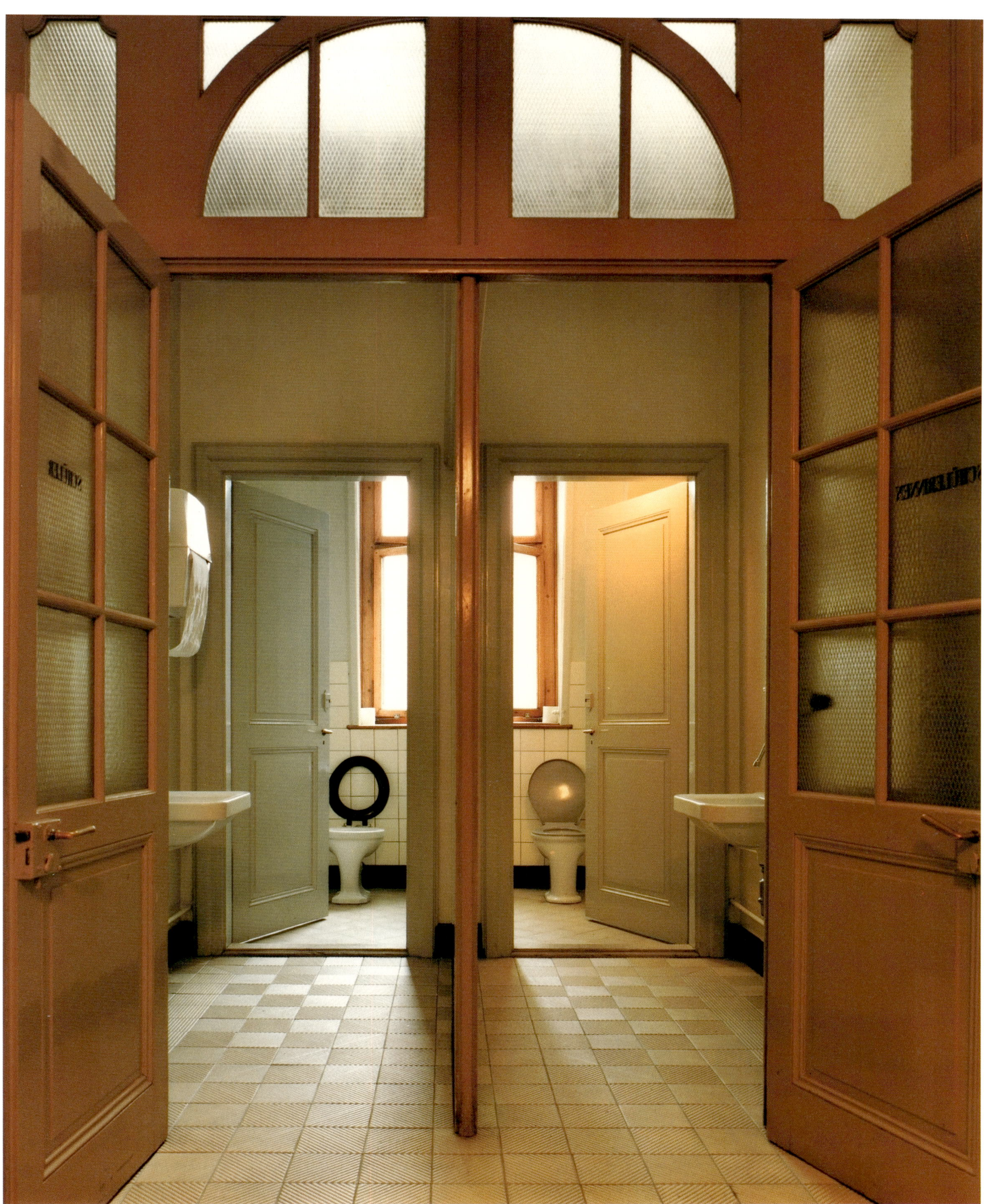

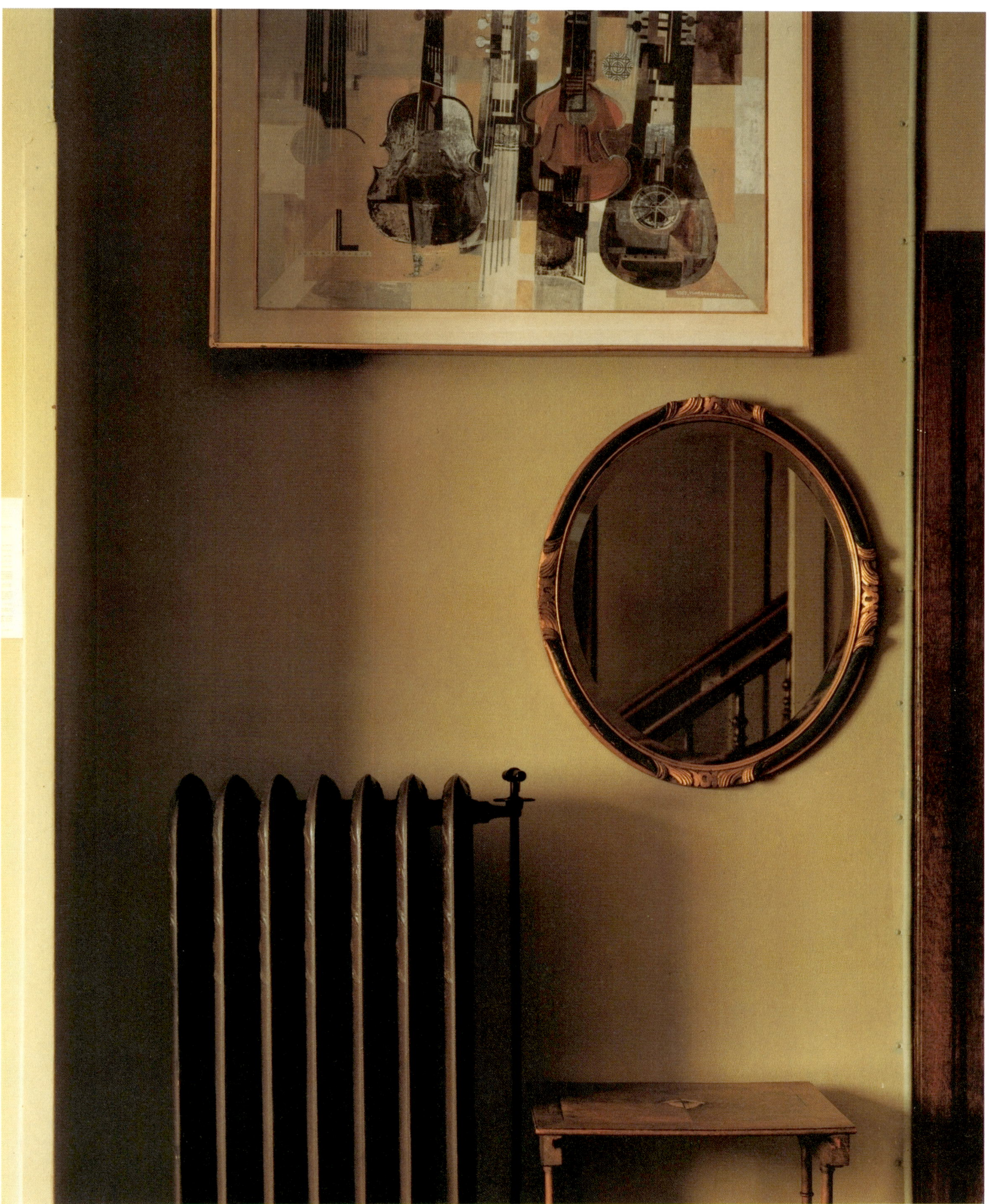

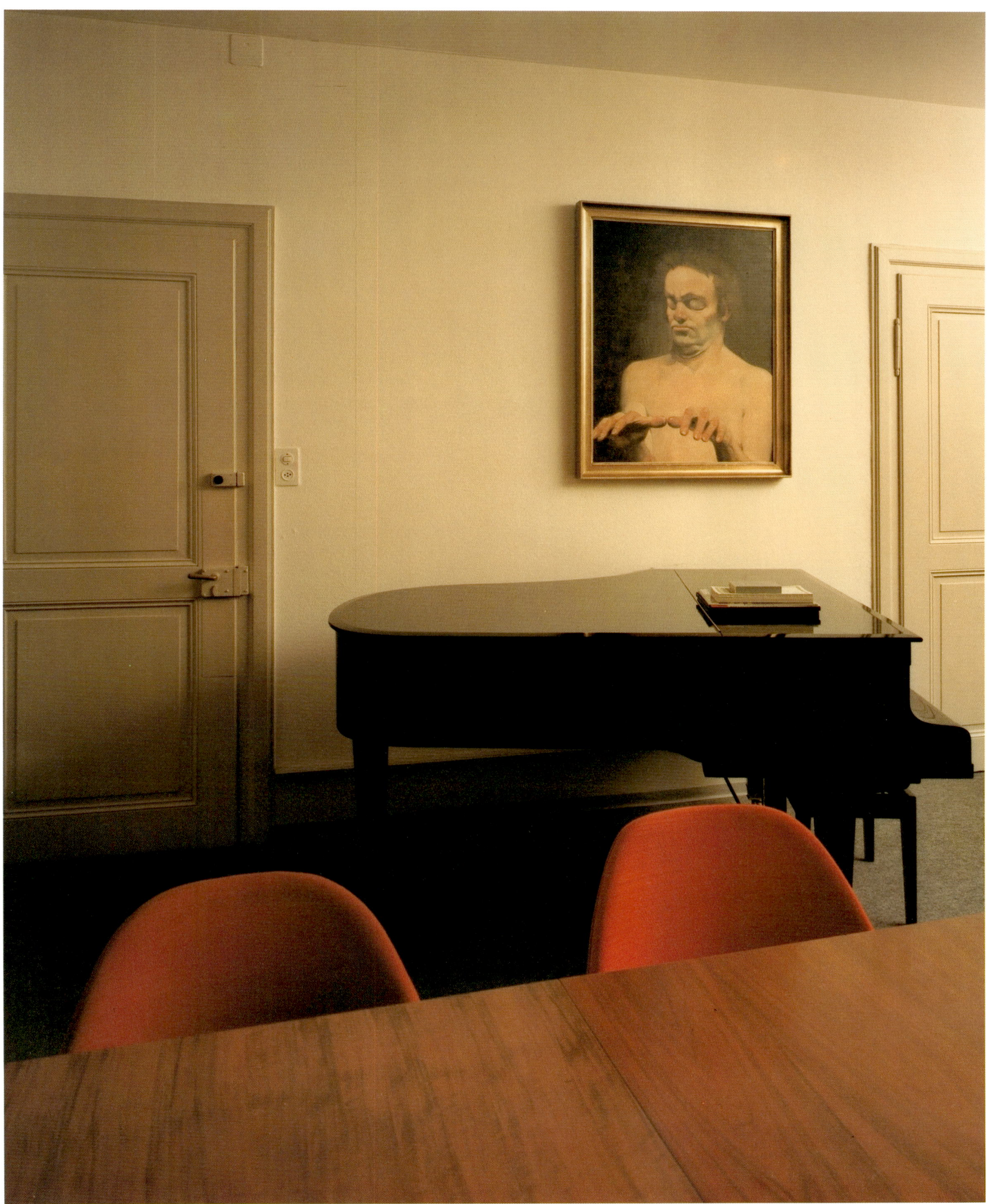

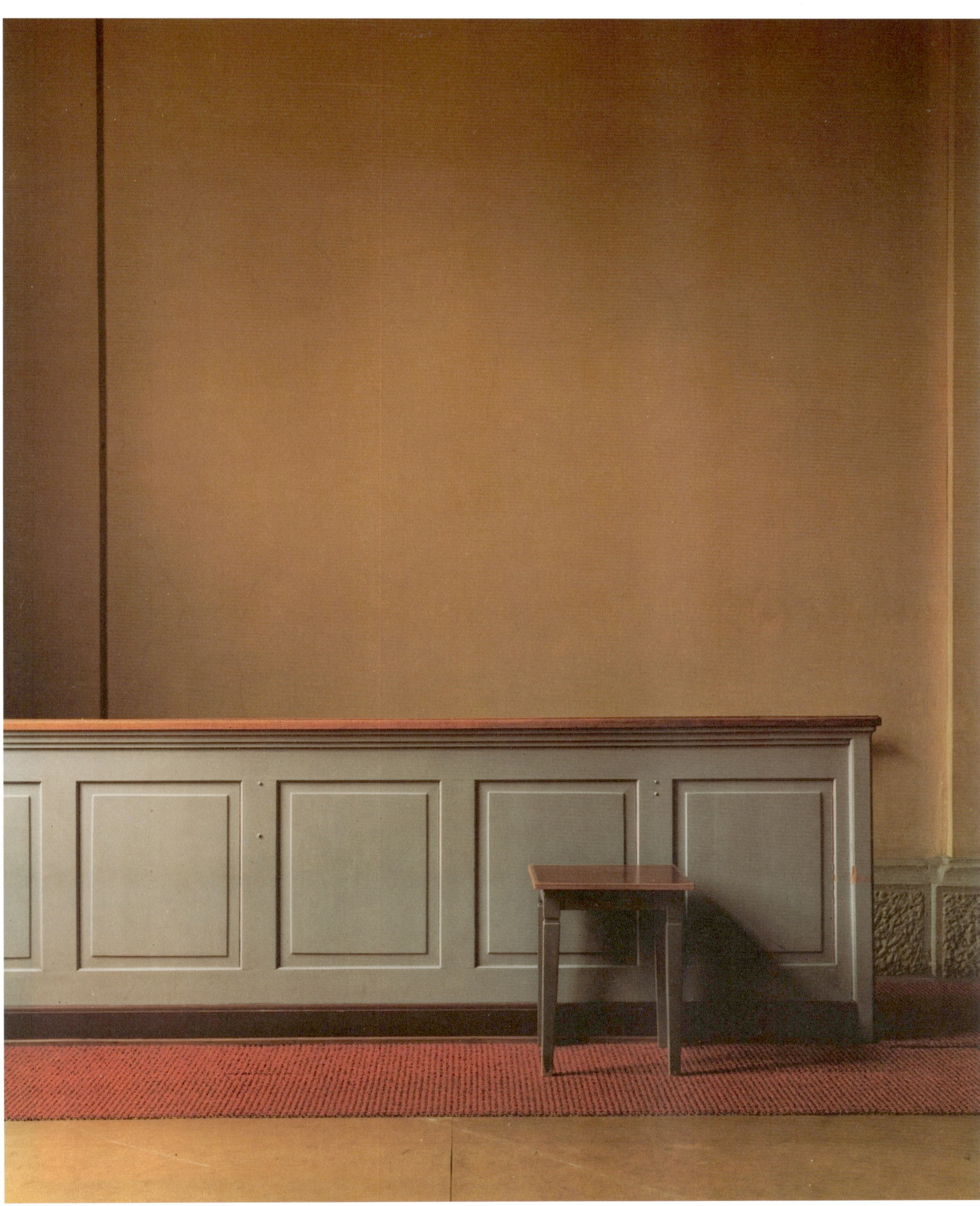

Images 1982

"I took these photographs in the spring of 1982. Indoors, because at the time one wasn't able to work outdoors. Outdoors, the shots would have turned out differently. Actually, it is irrelevant whether indoors or outdoors – irrelevant, how these things come together – it only matters that the outer and the inner things do meet. Based upon this work, I shall know later on, where I was today."

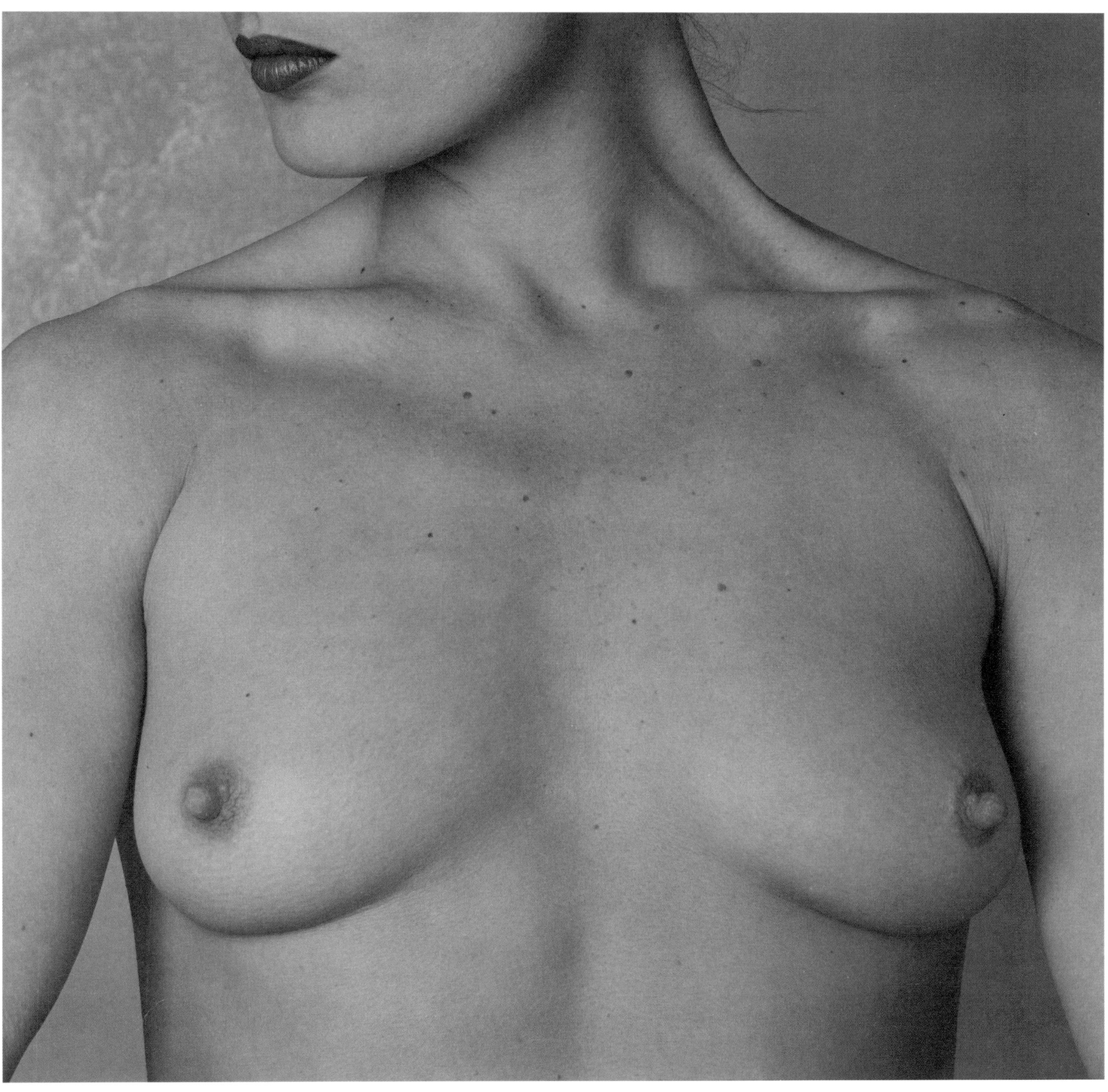

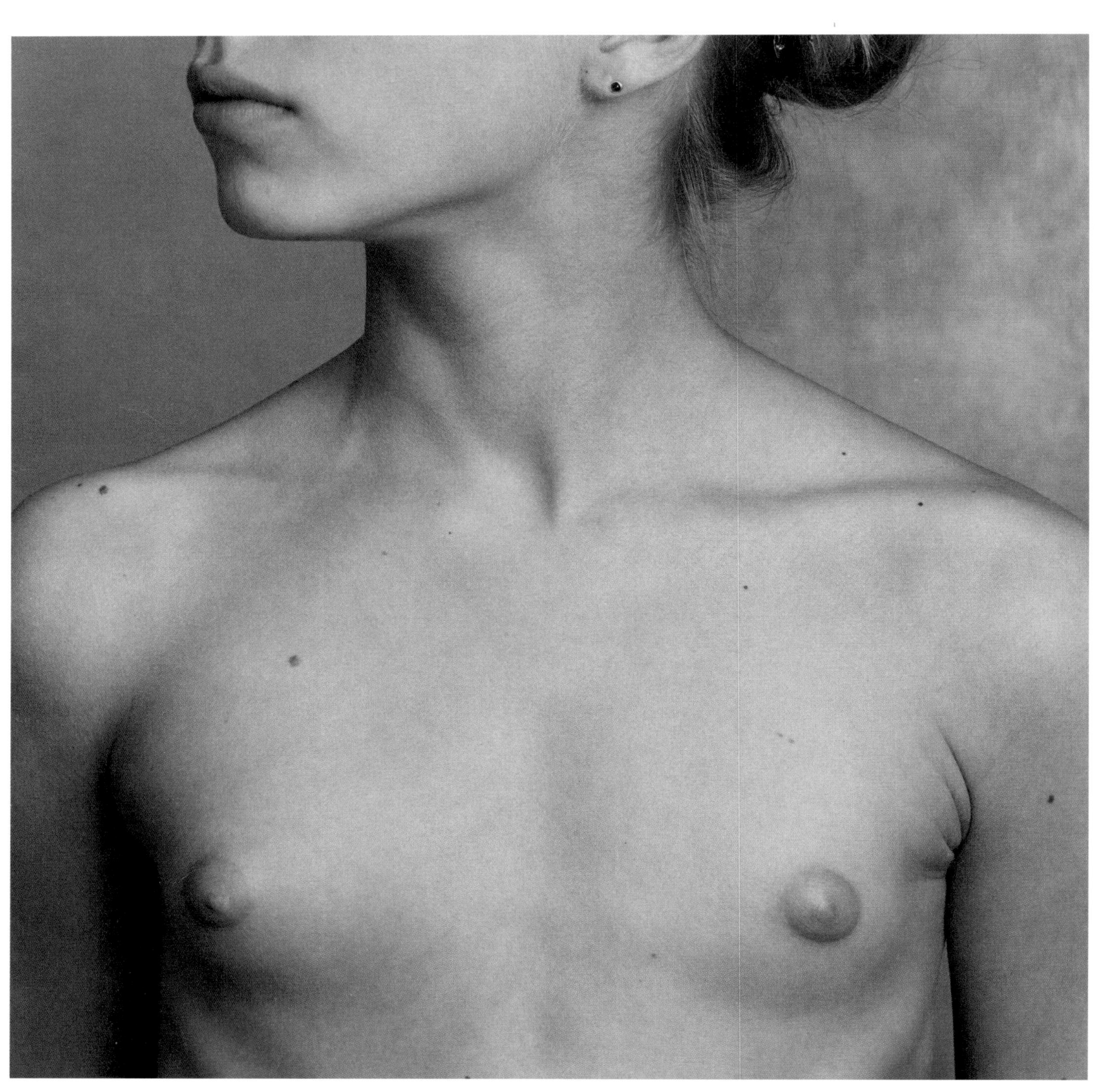

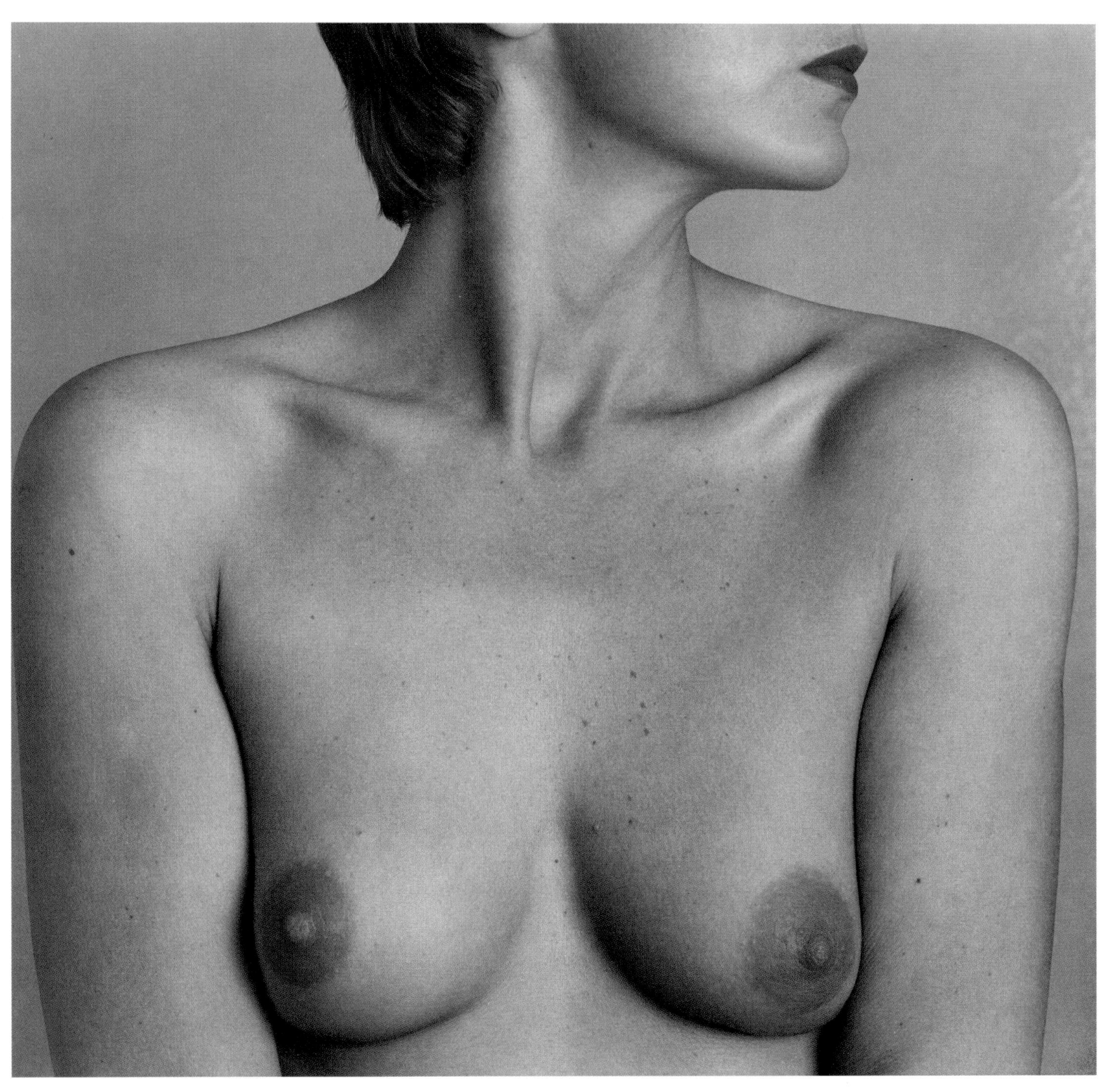

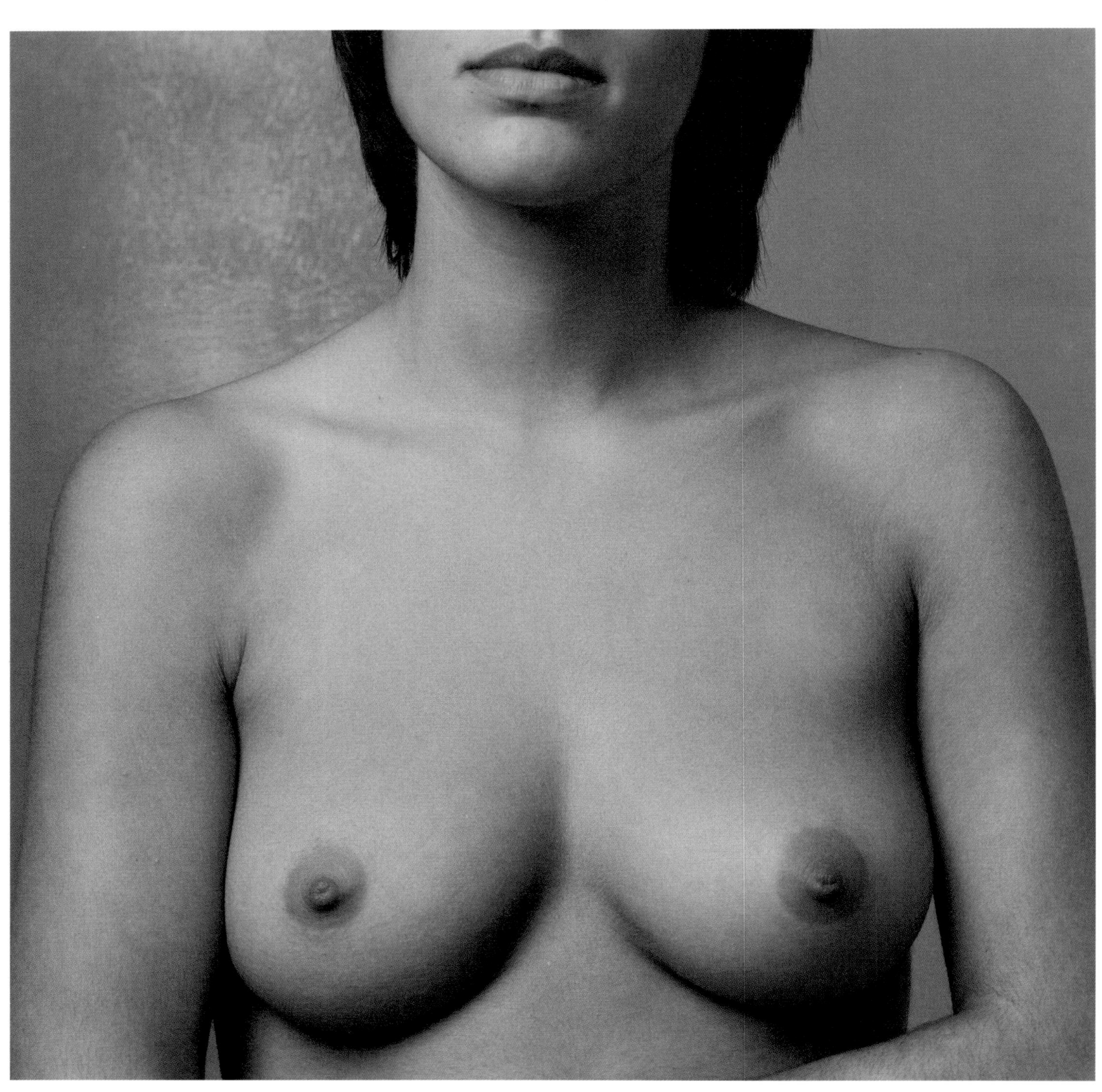

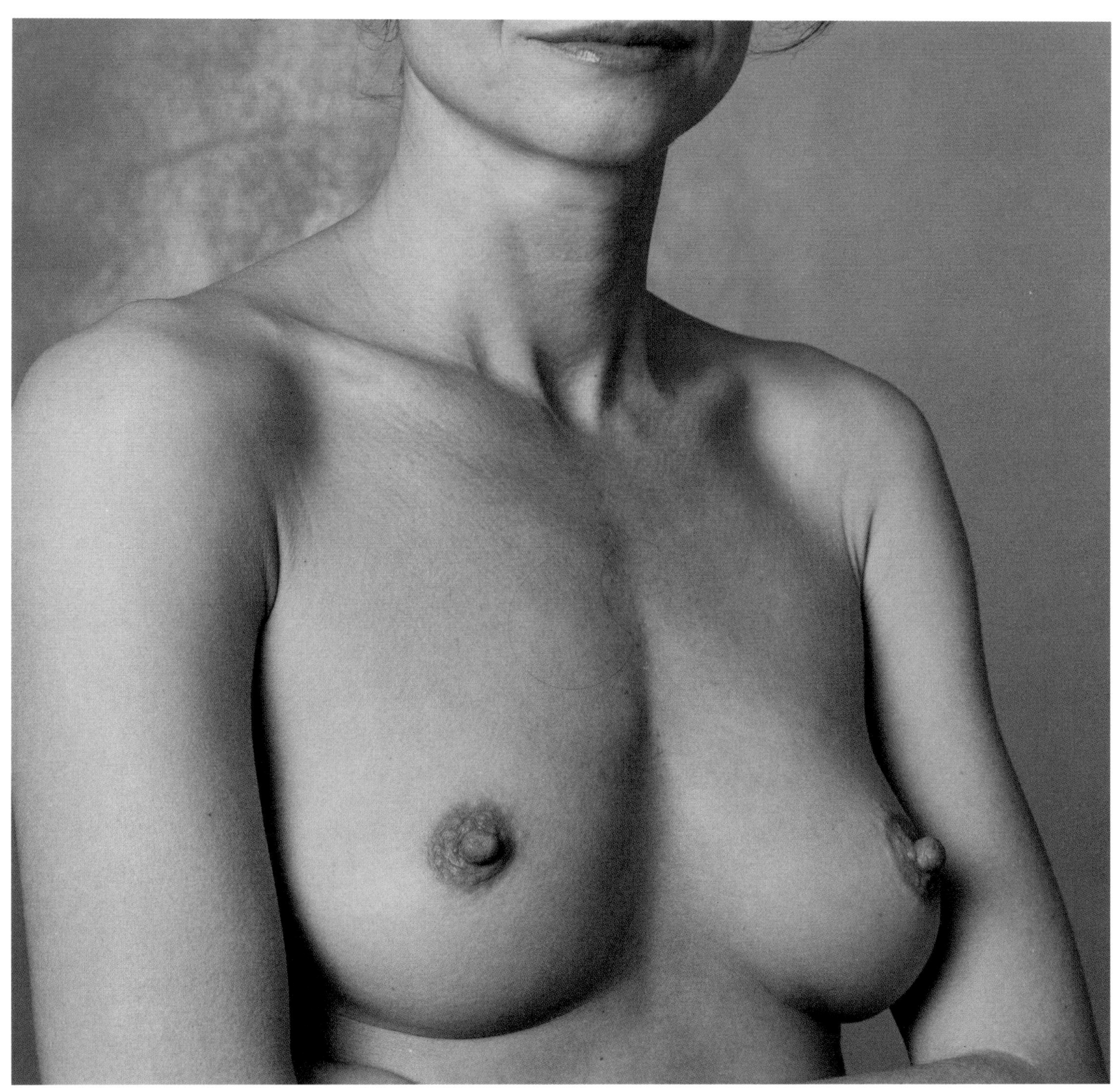

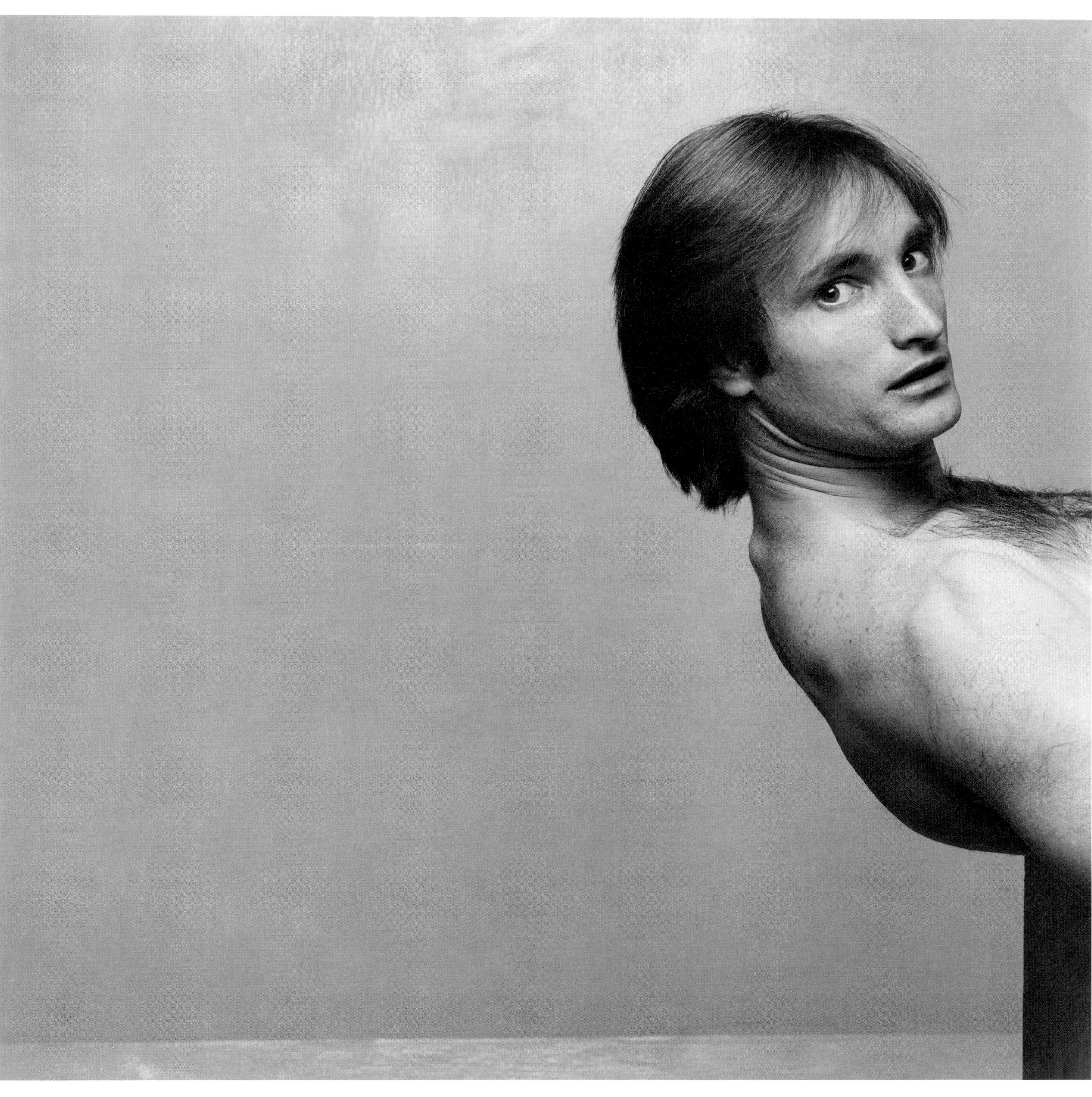

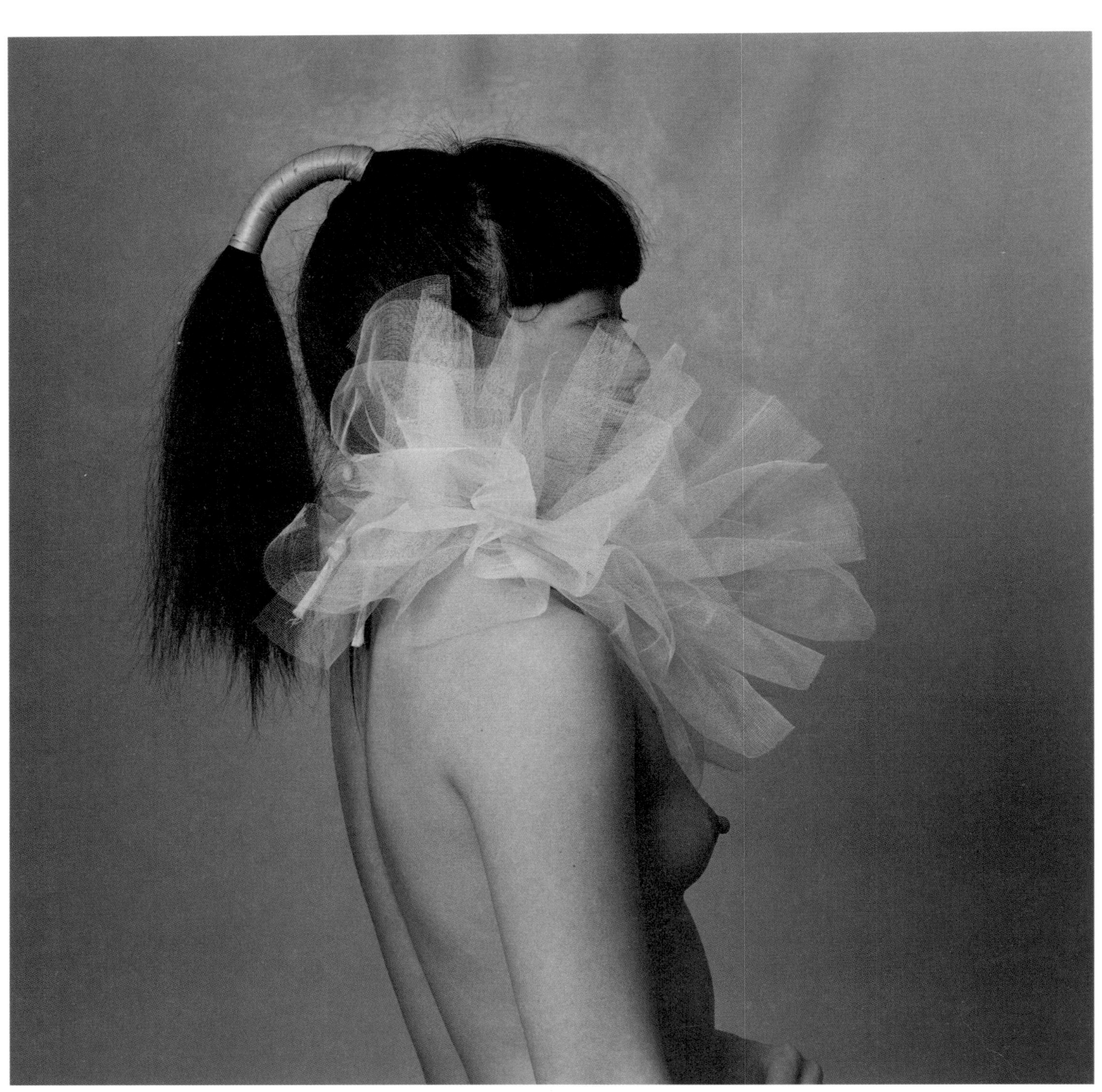

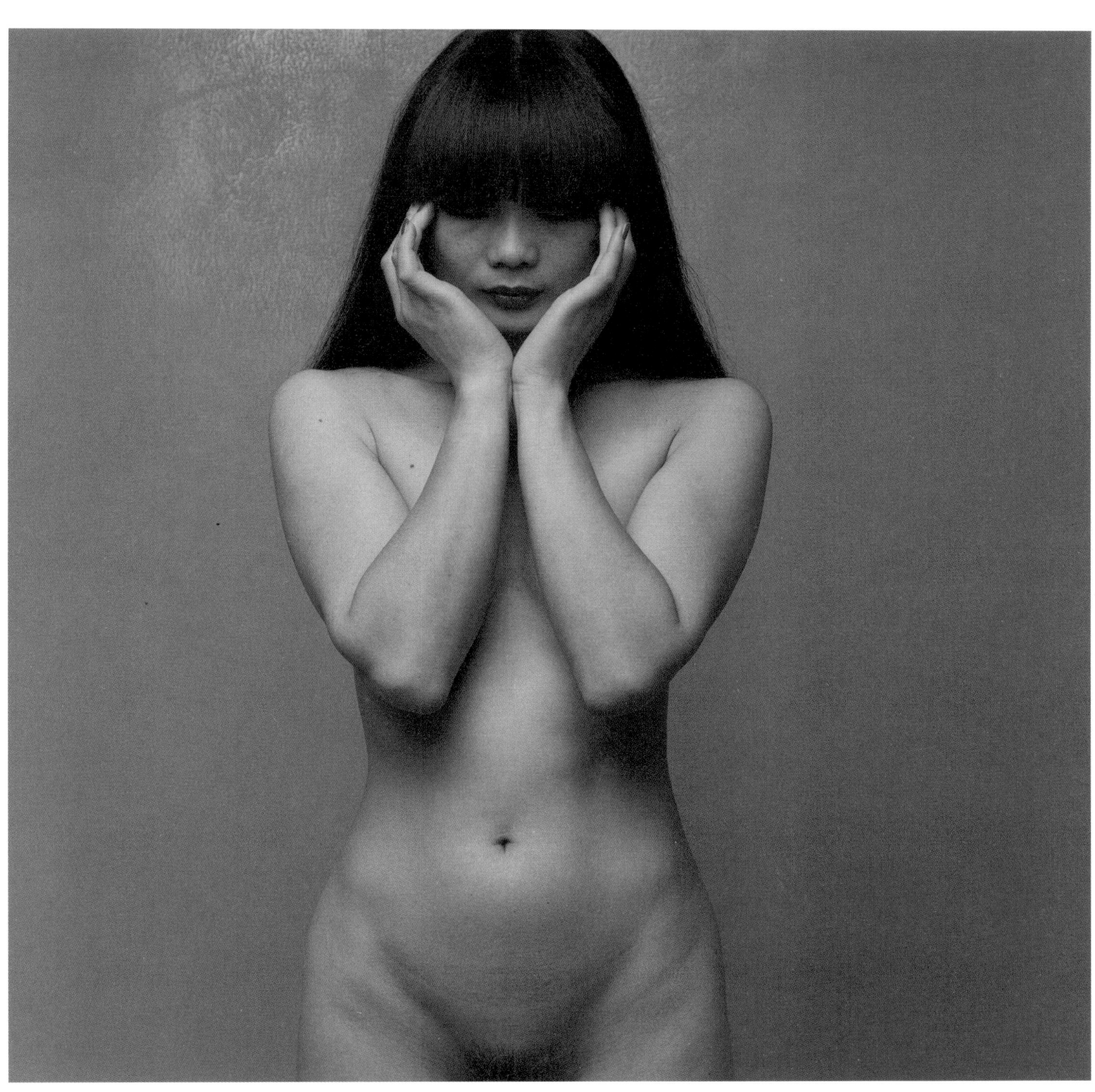

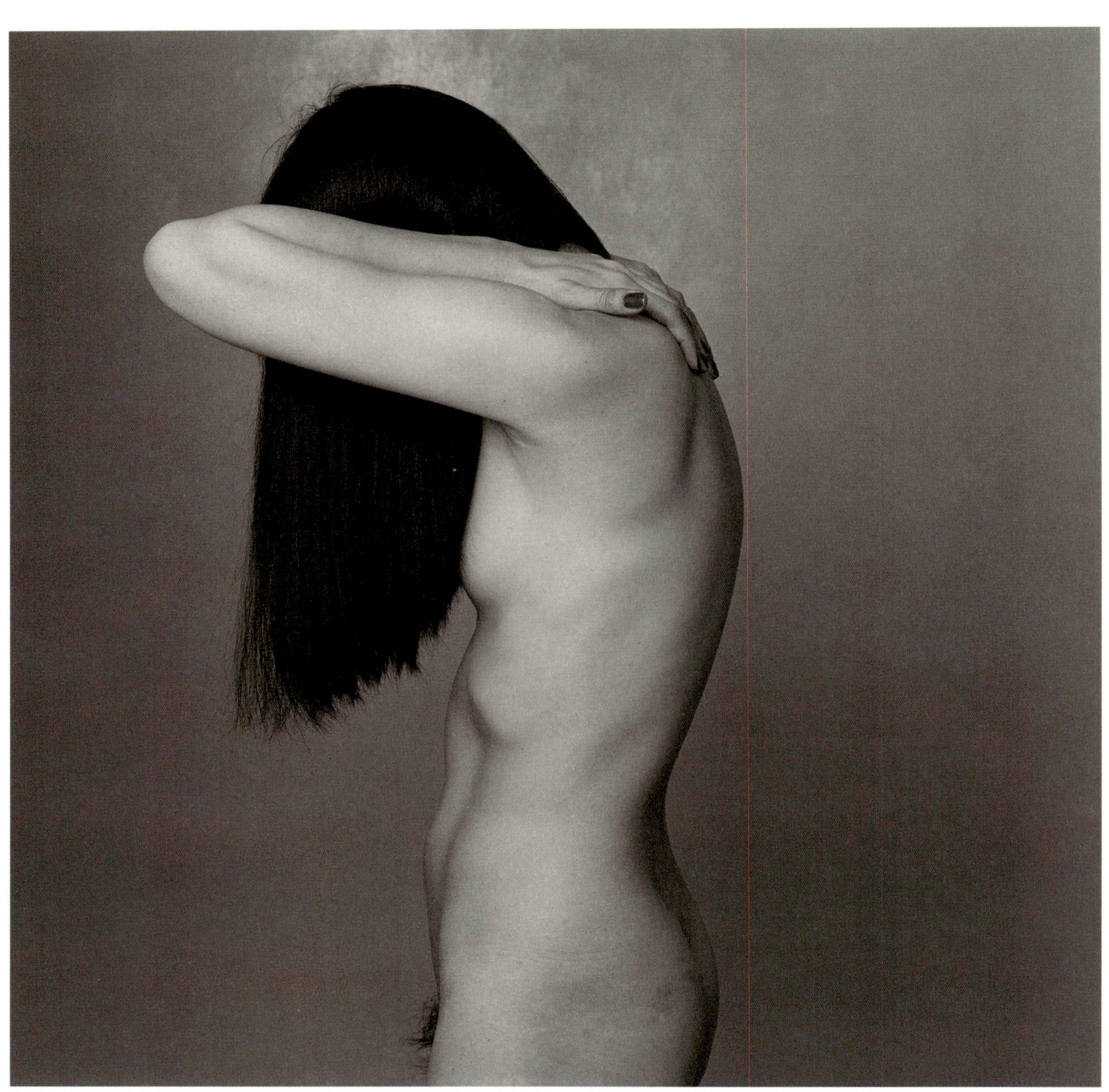

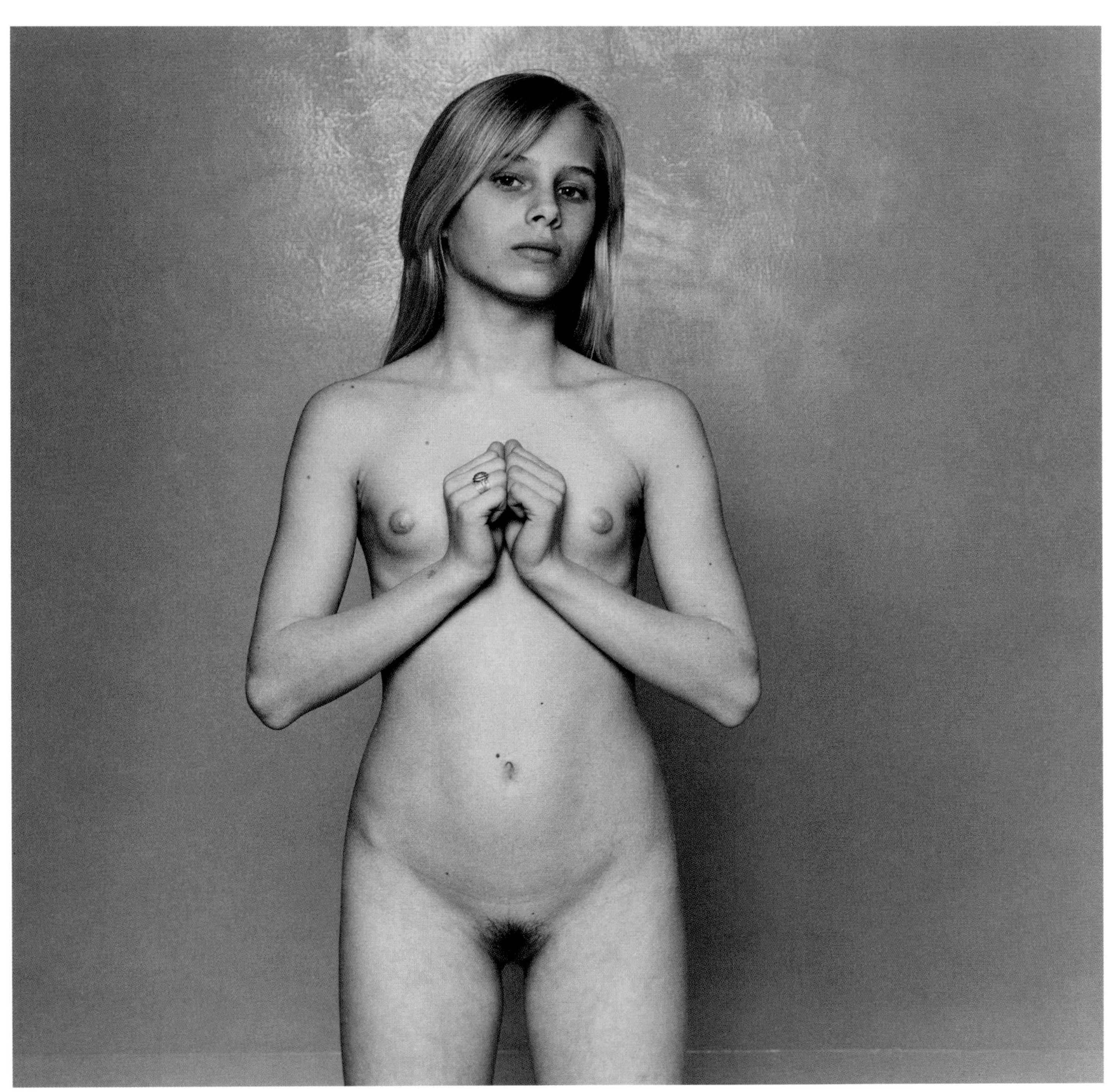

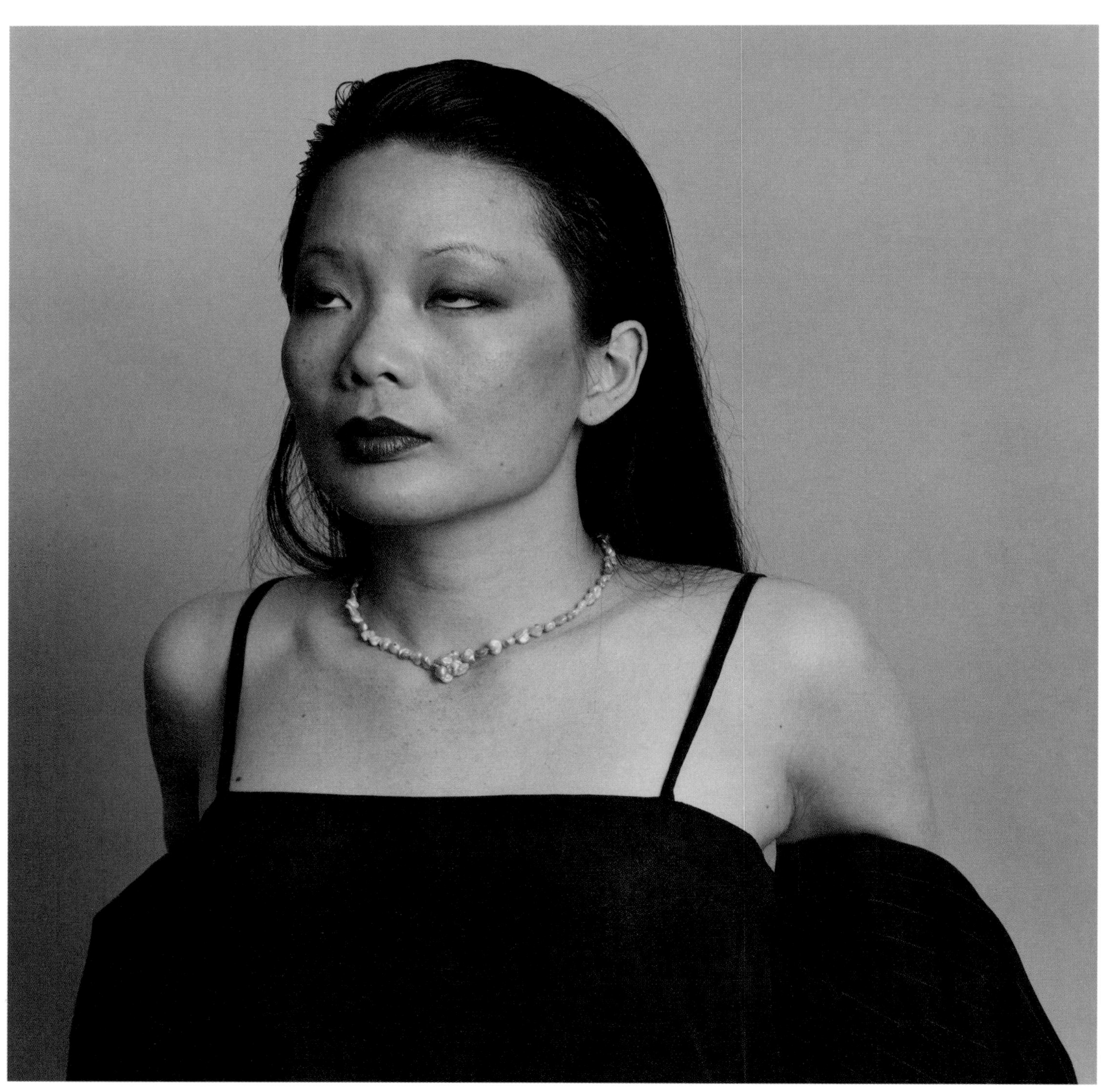

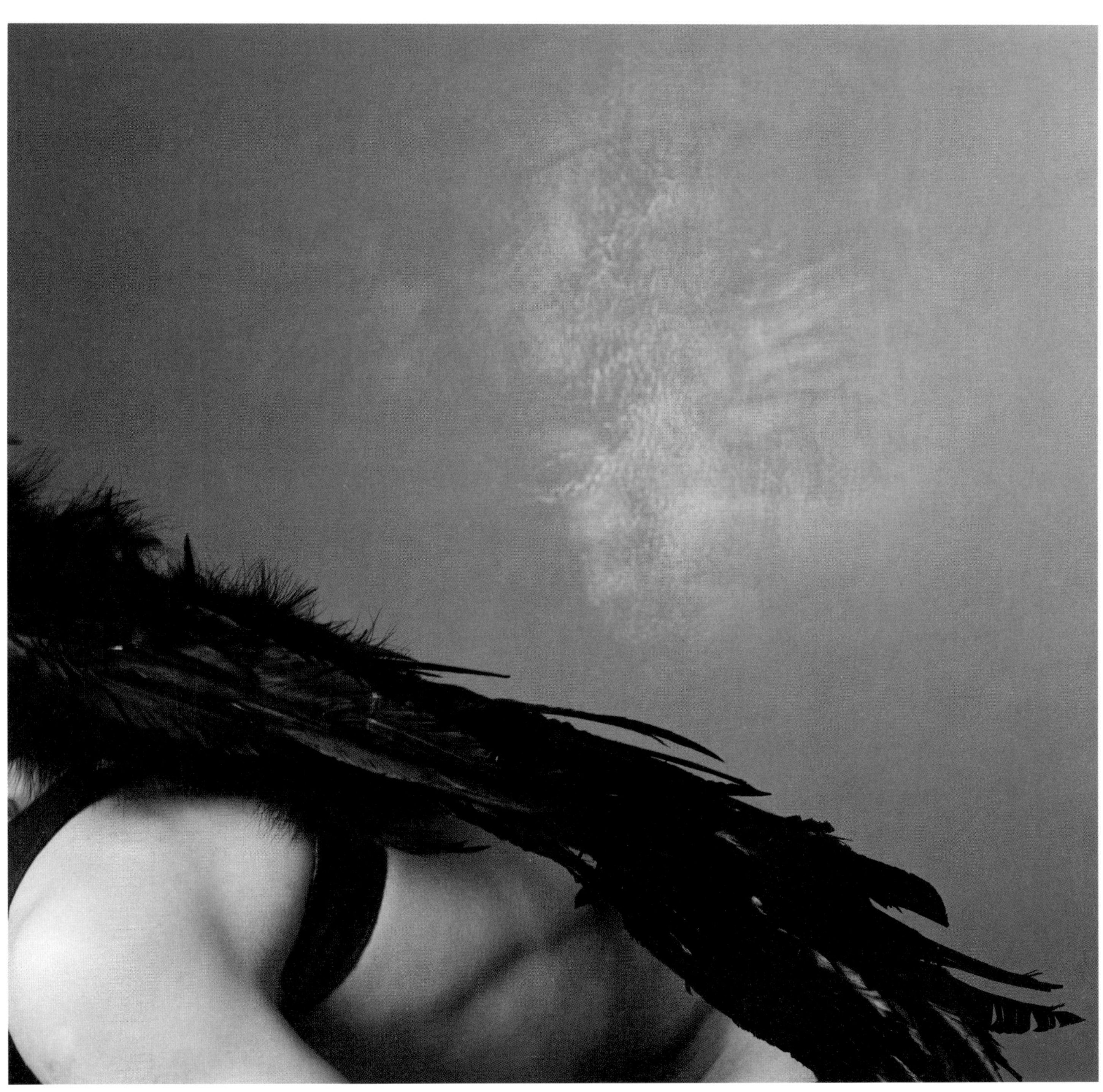

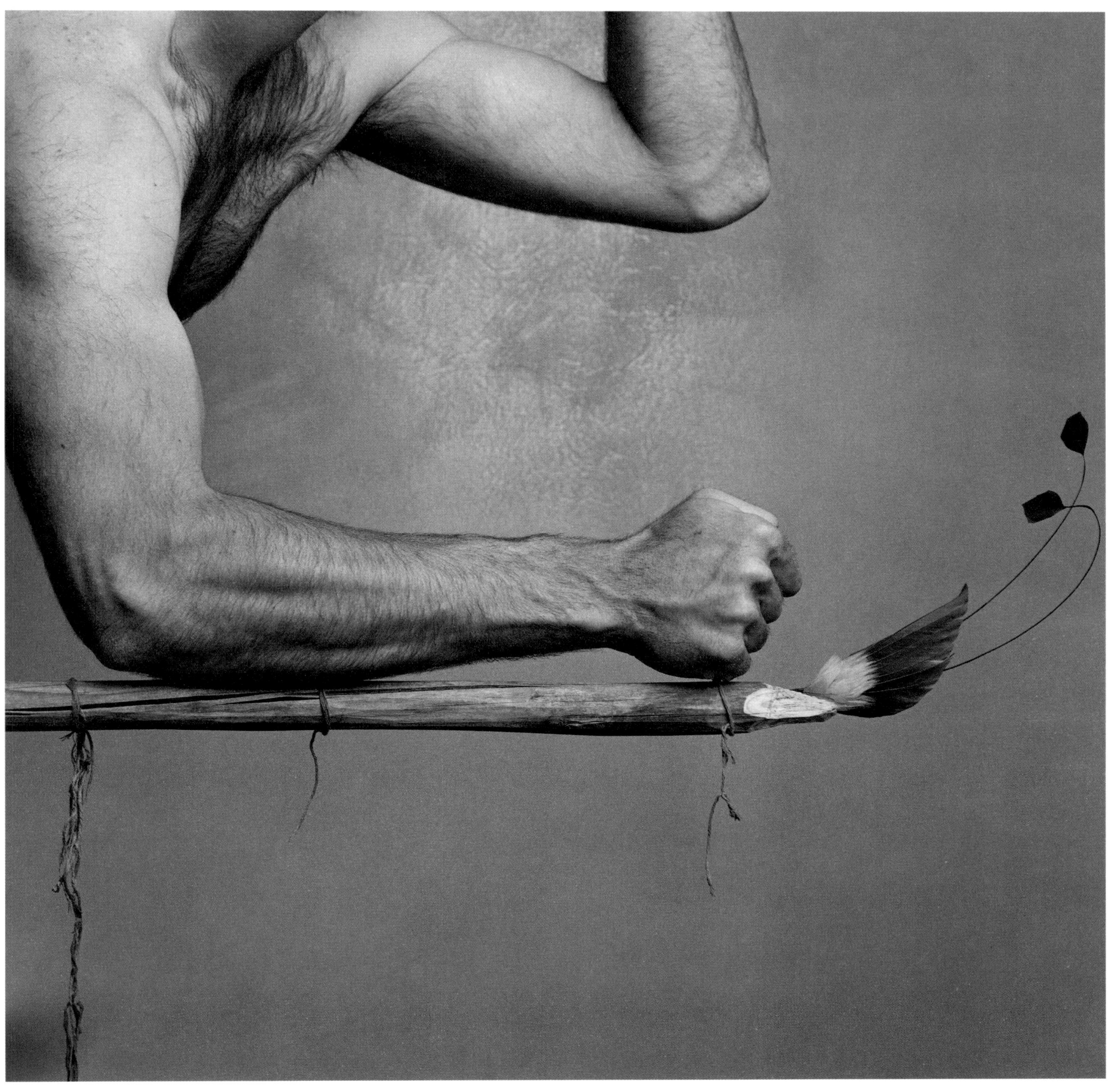

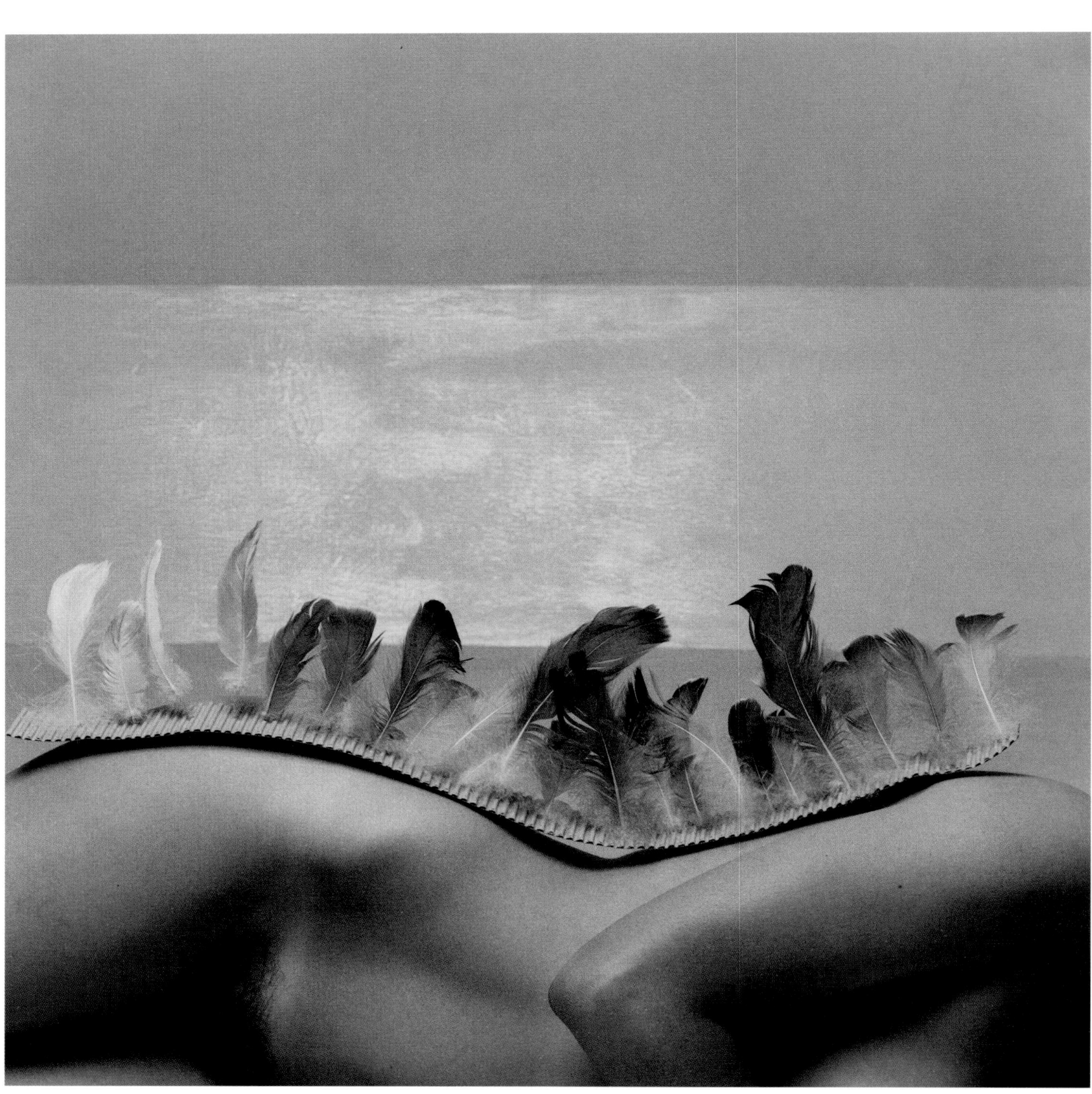

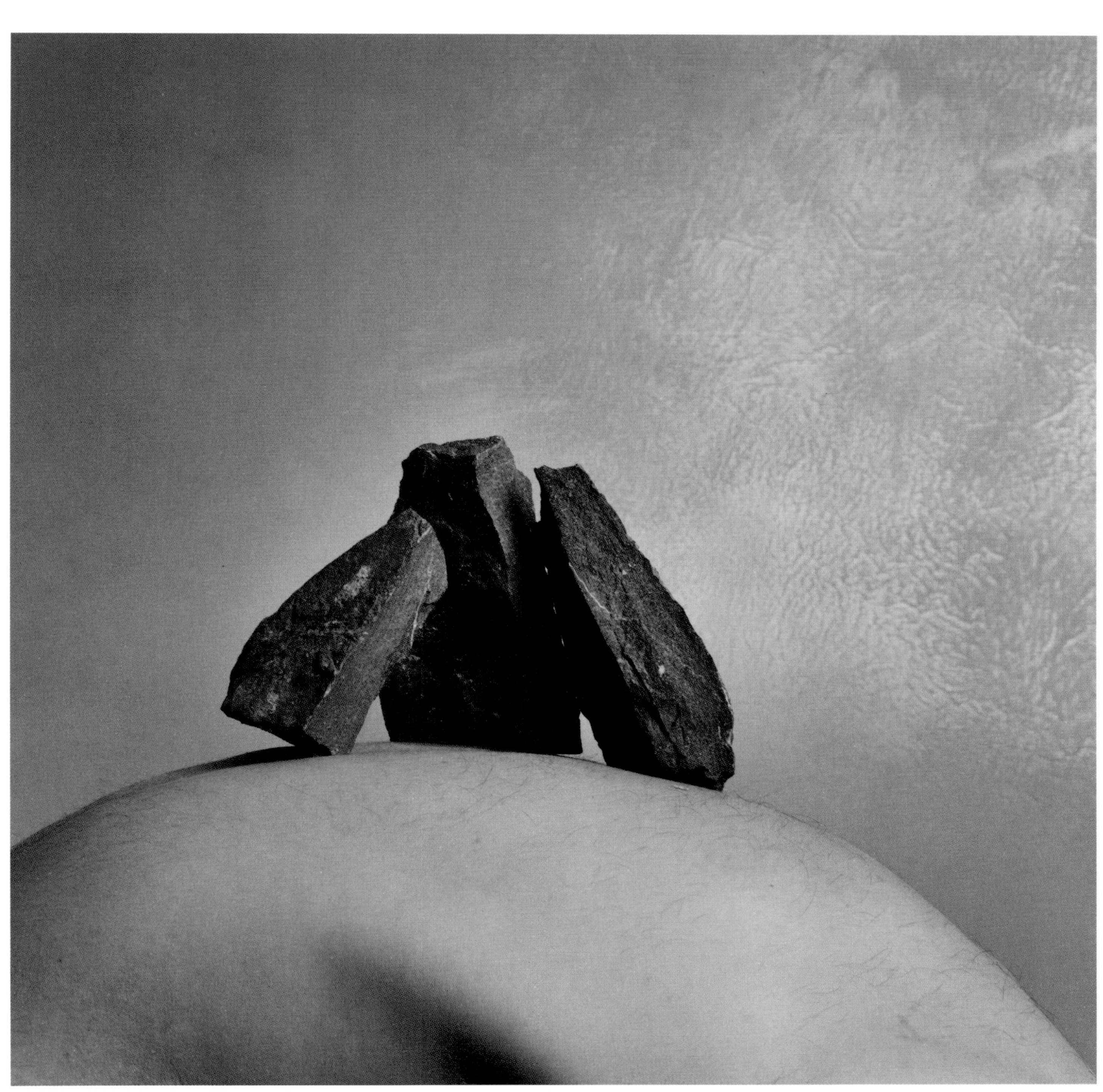

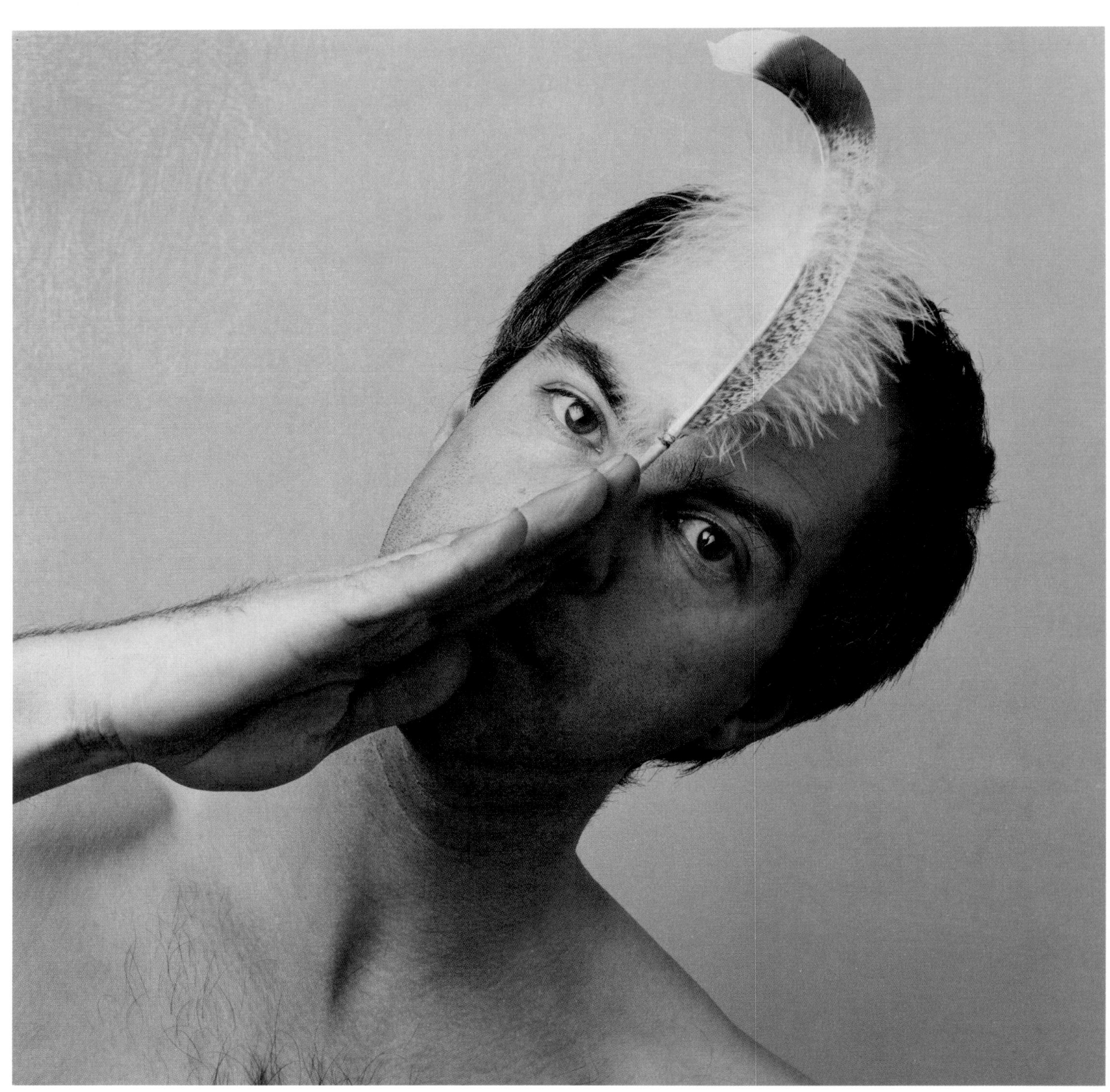

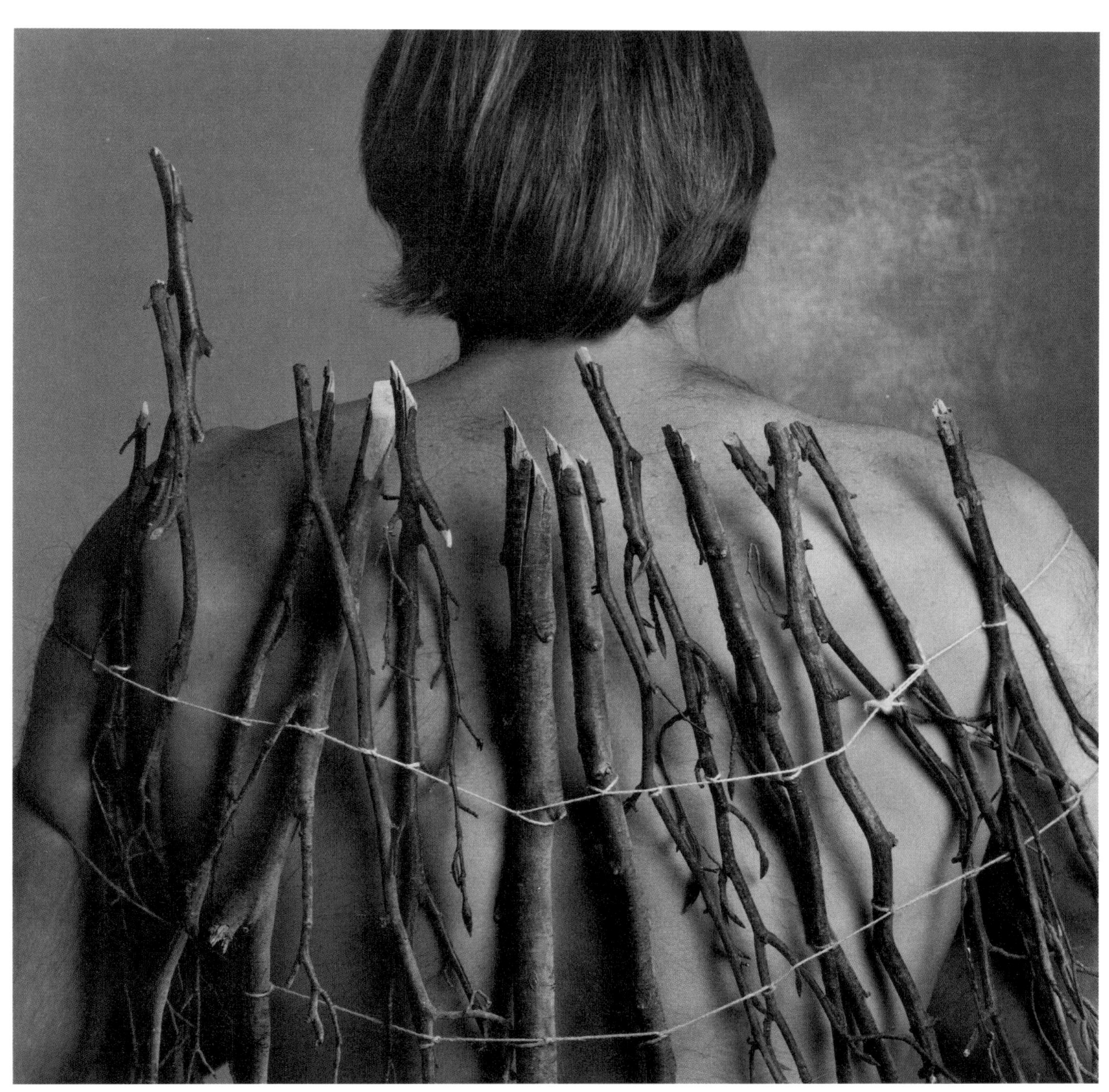

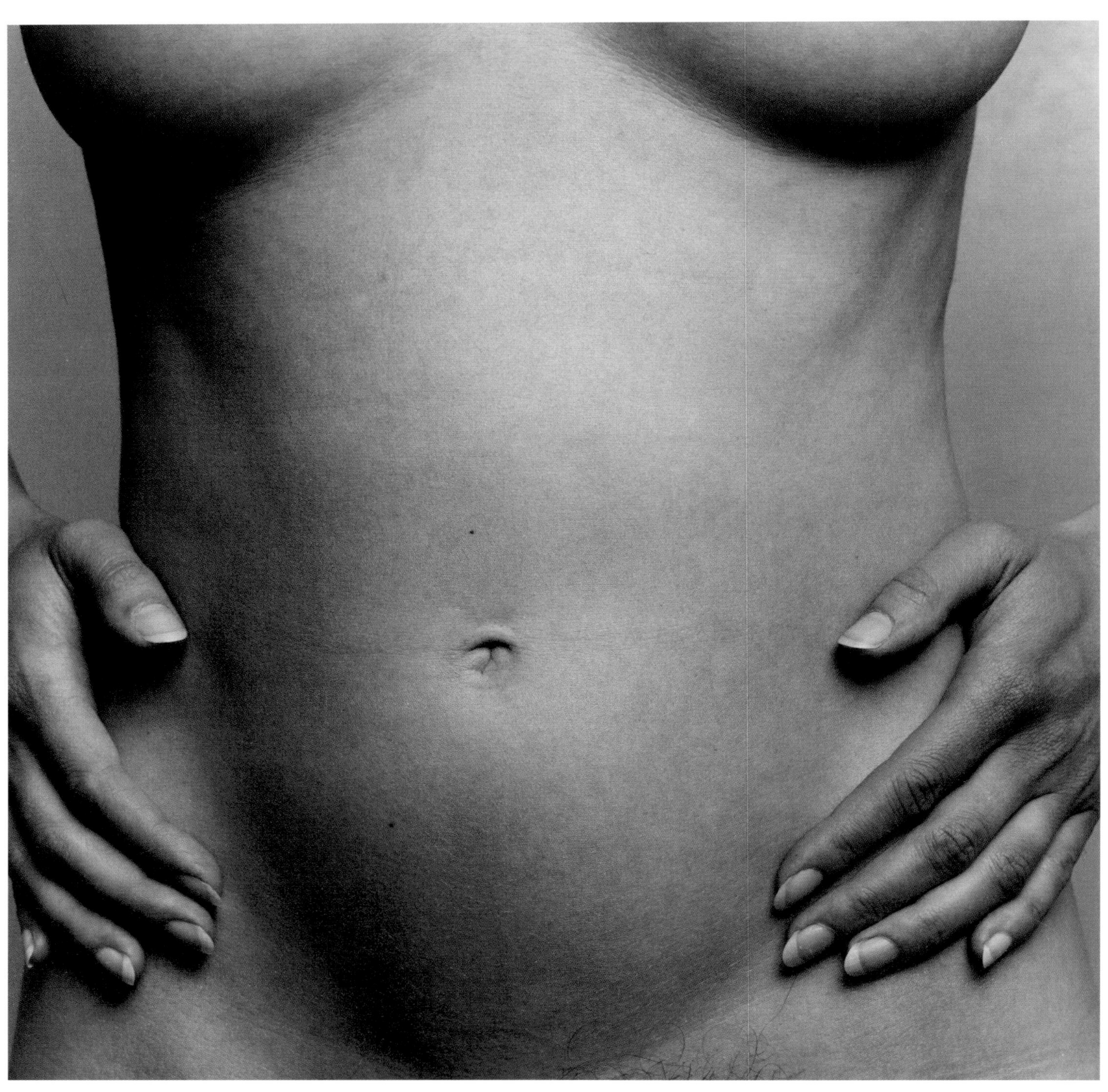

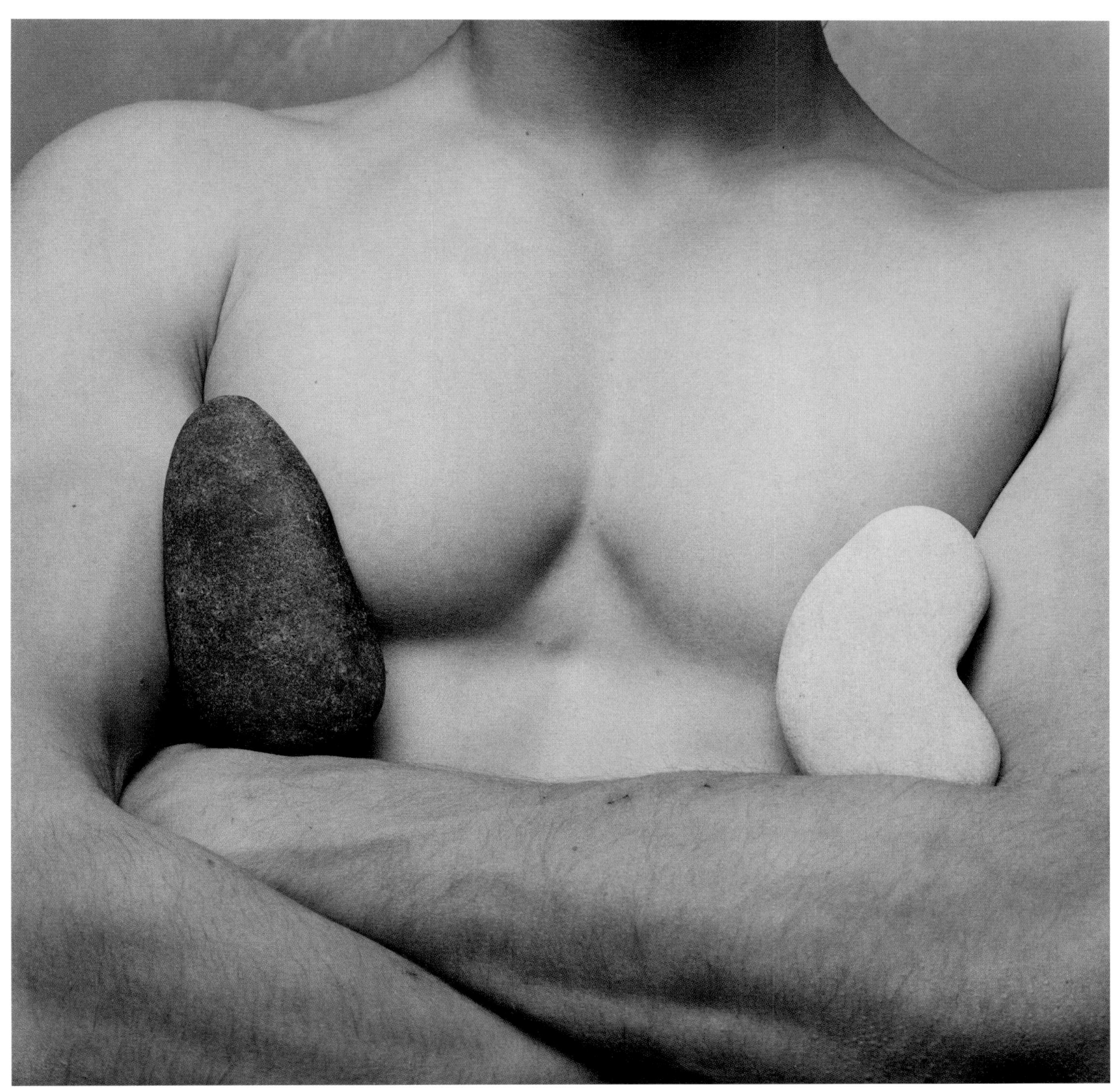

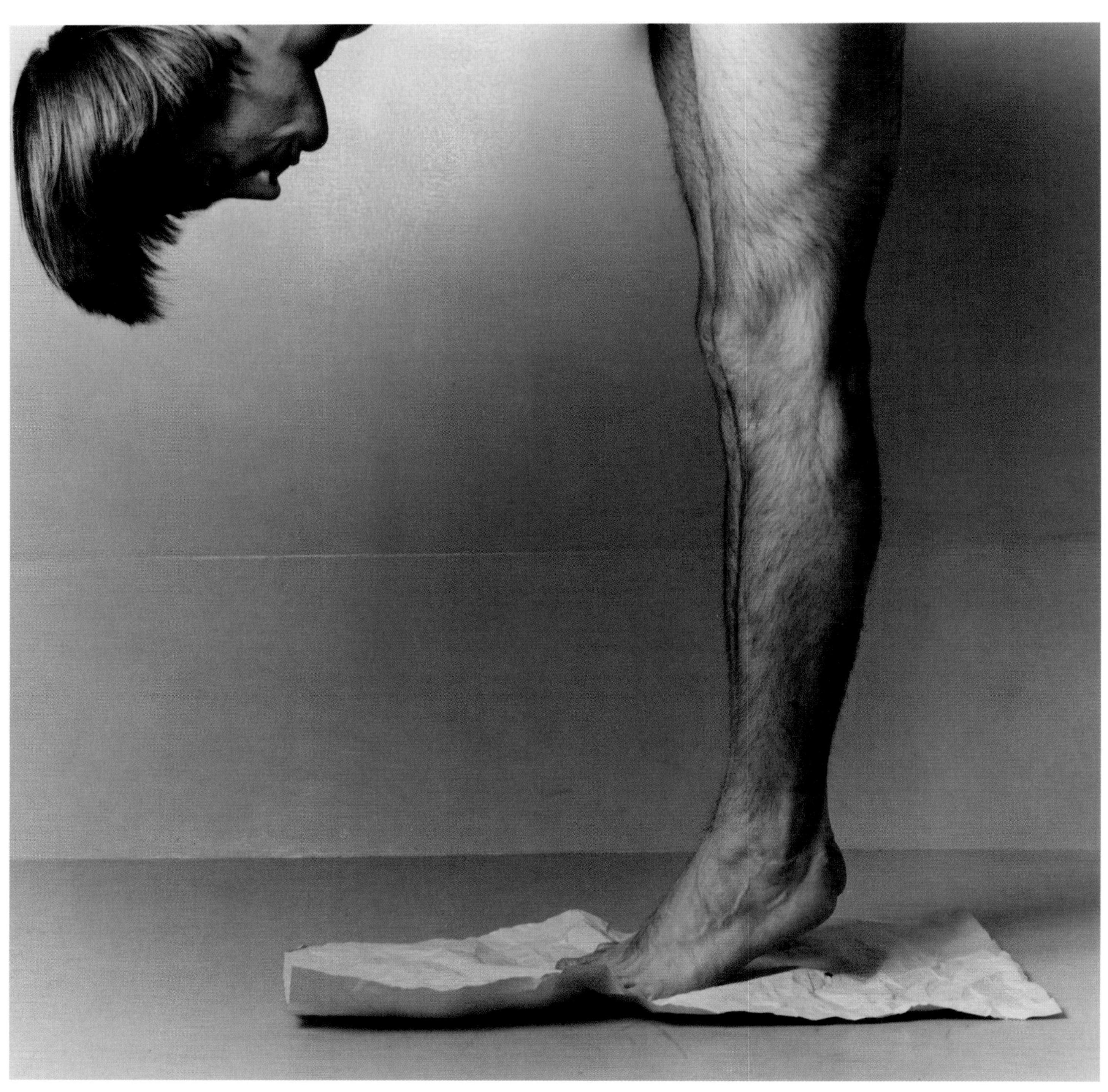

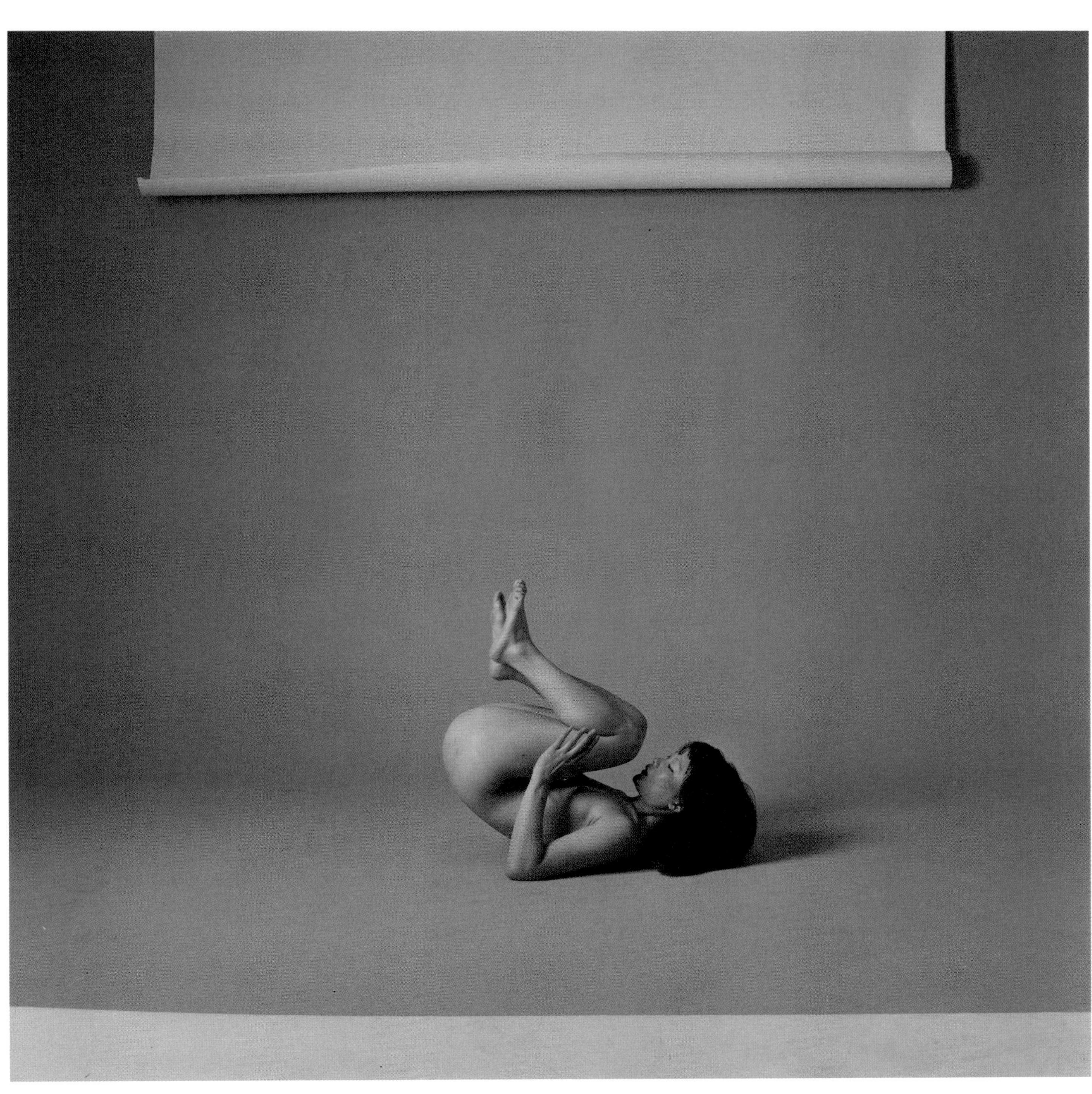

Onlookers 1977
''The idea for 'Onlookers' came after I had returned from two photographically unsatisfactory trips to India.

Time and again on raising my camera I had the intolerable feeling that my 'sujets' were completely cliché-ridden.

On my third trip however, to create the contrast to the Indian background, I always used a western viewer.

An idea which I have continued to follow.''

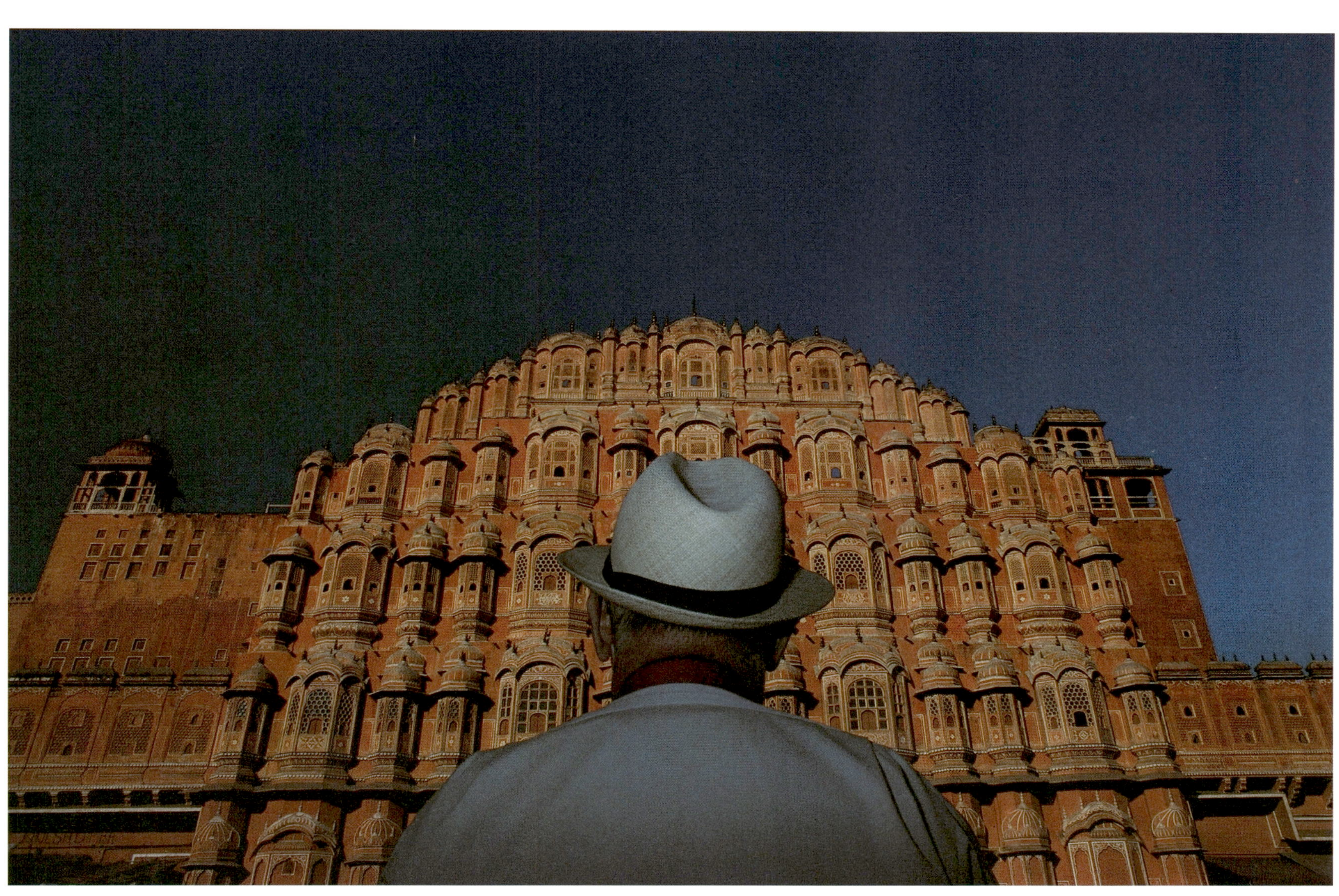

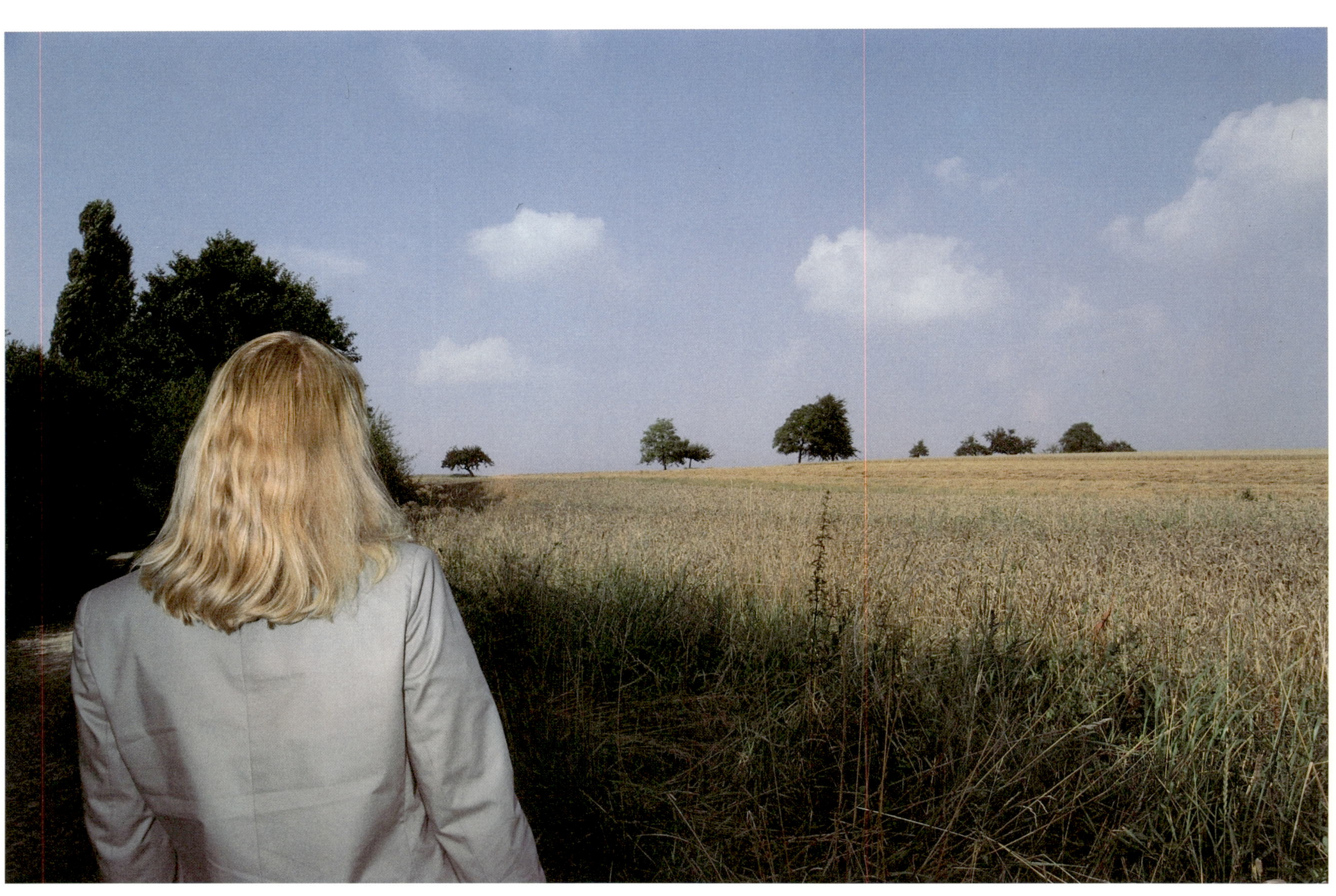

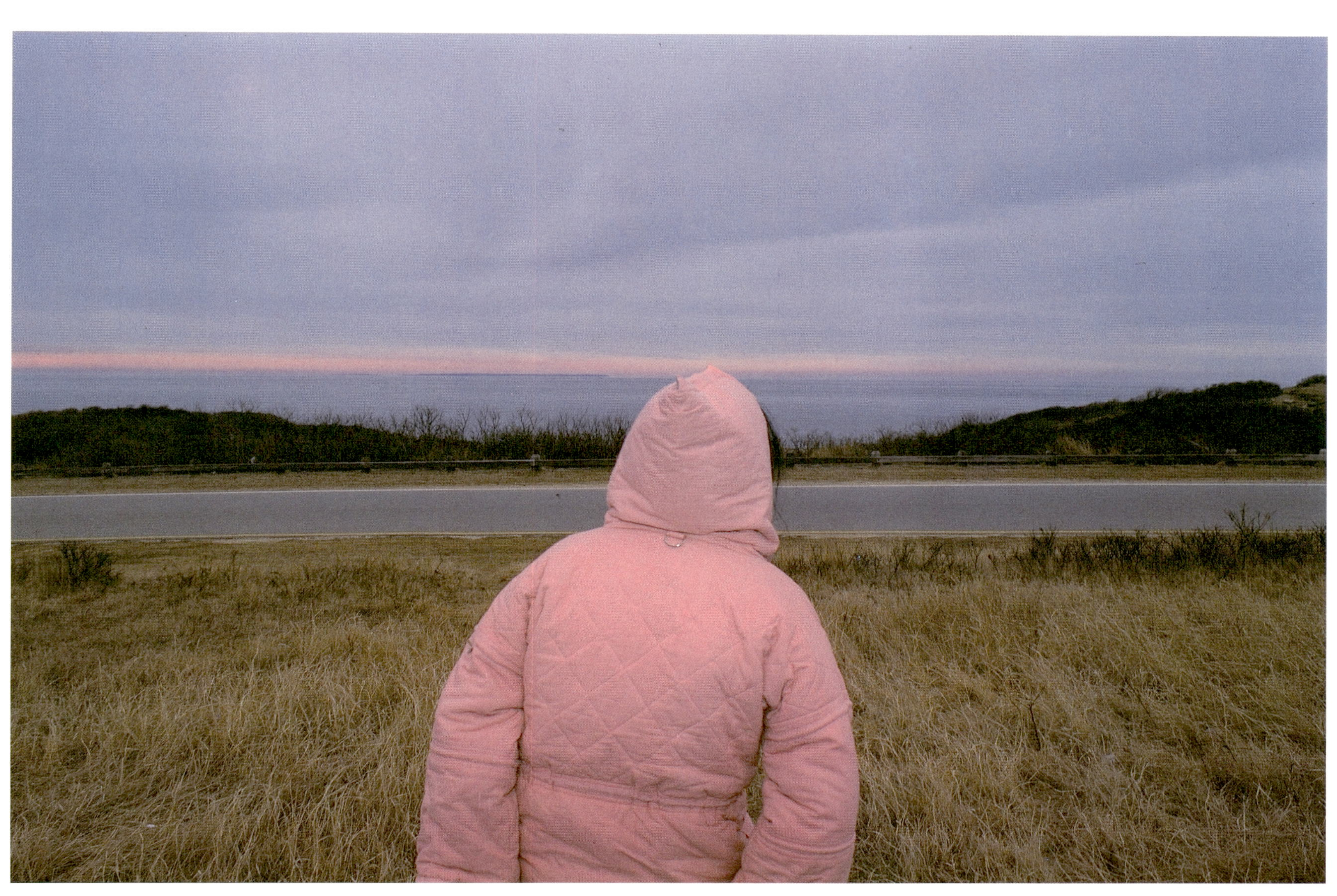

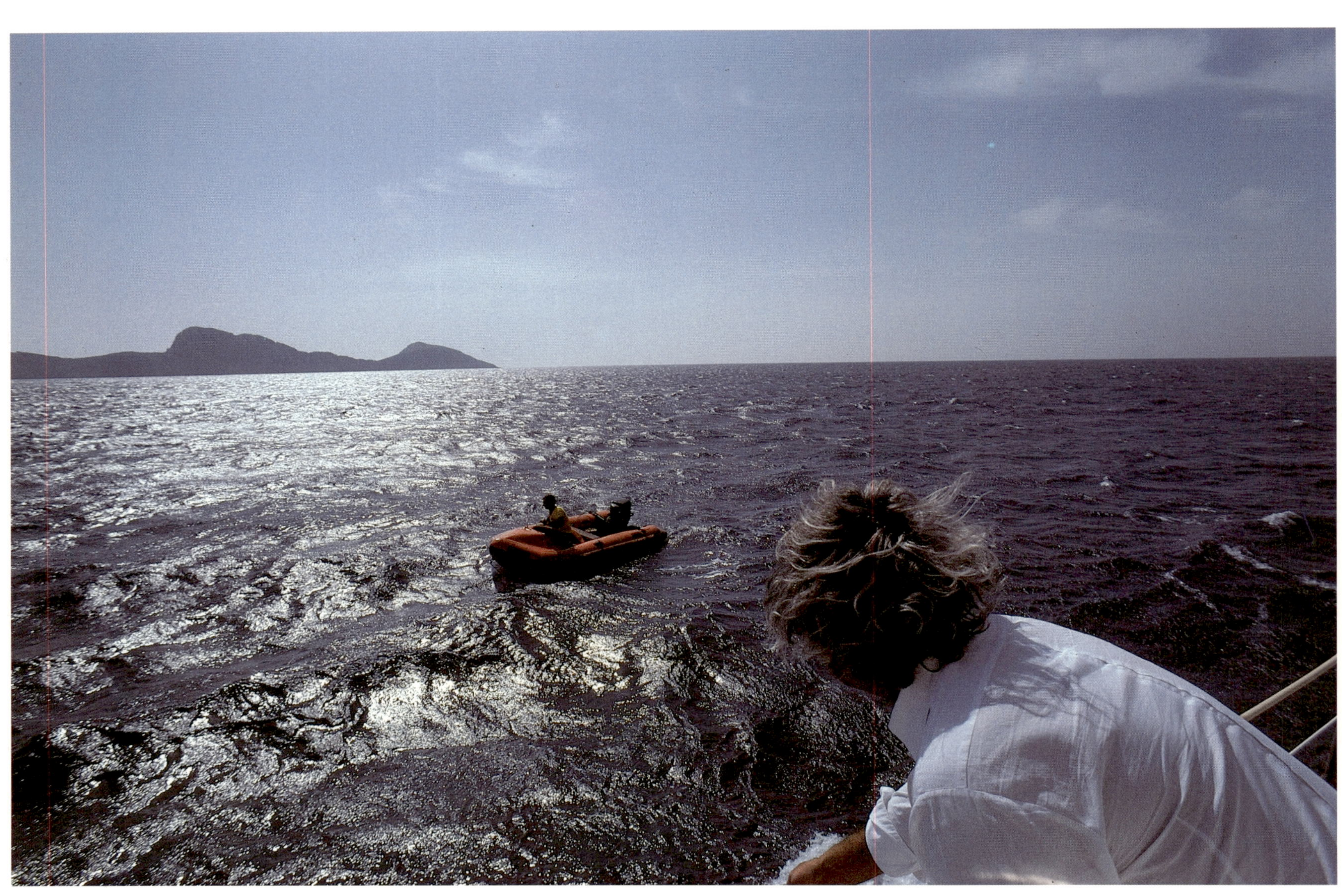

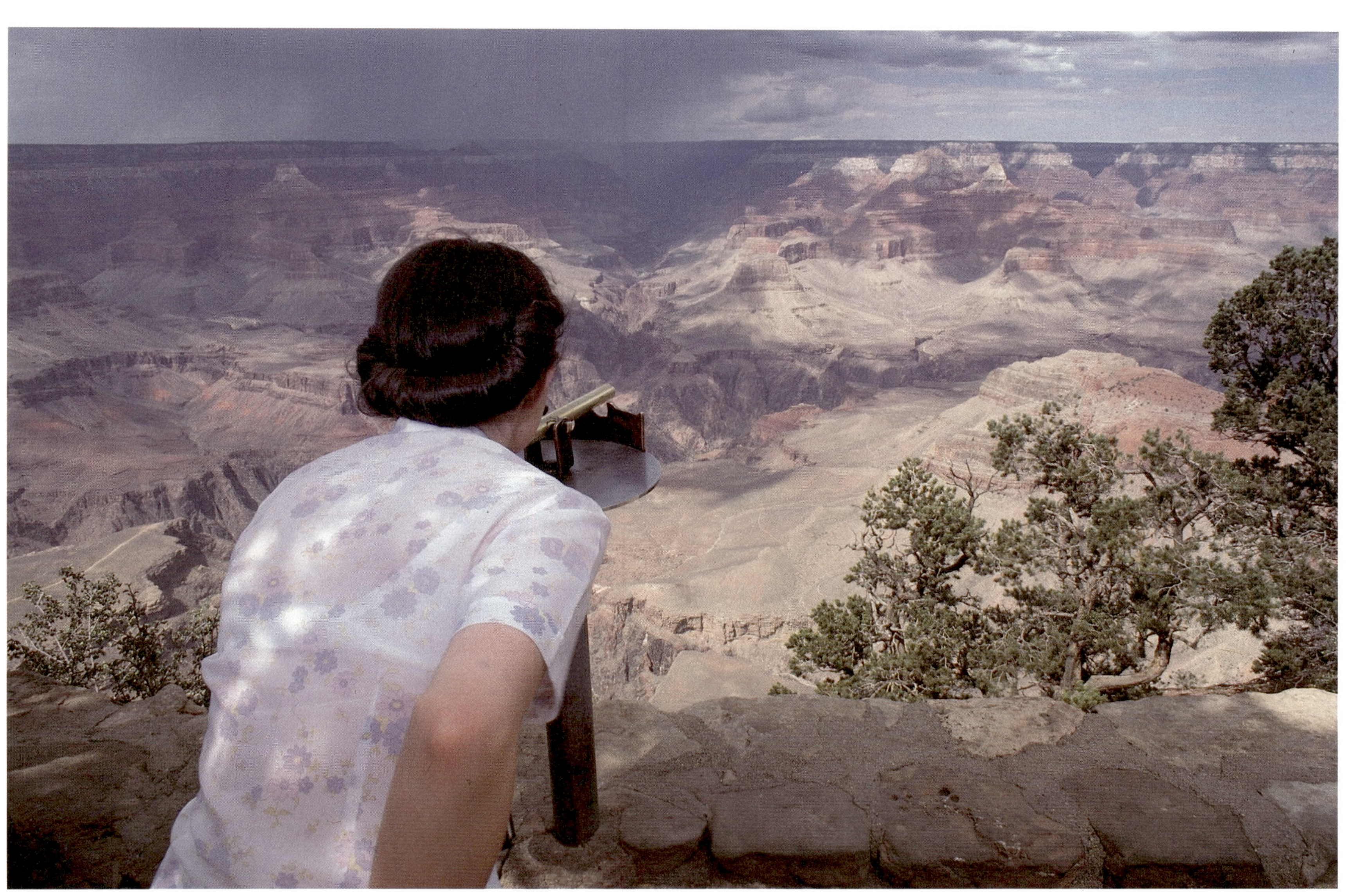

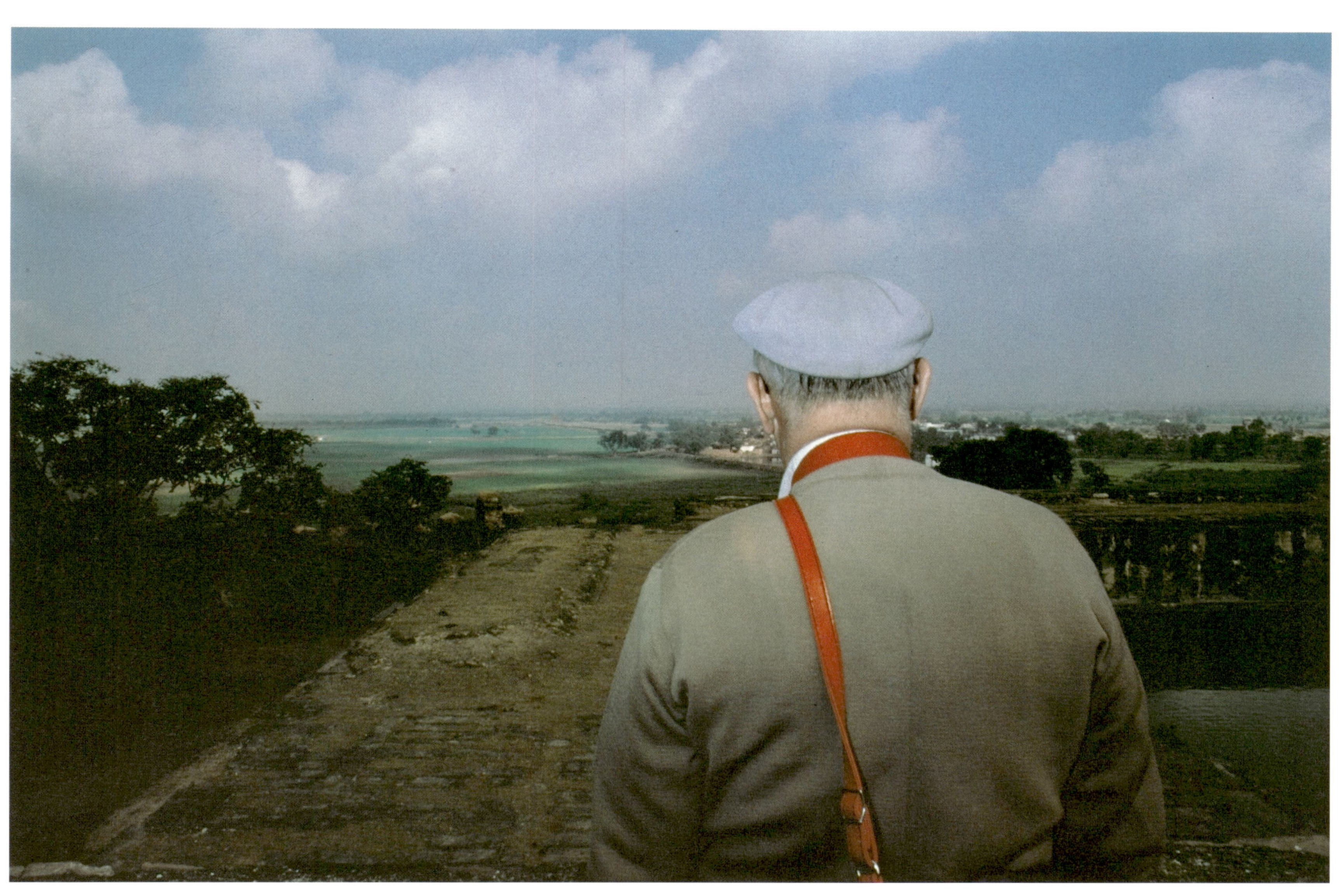

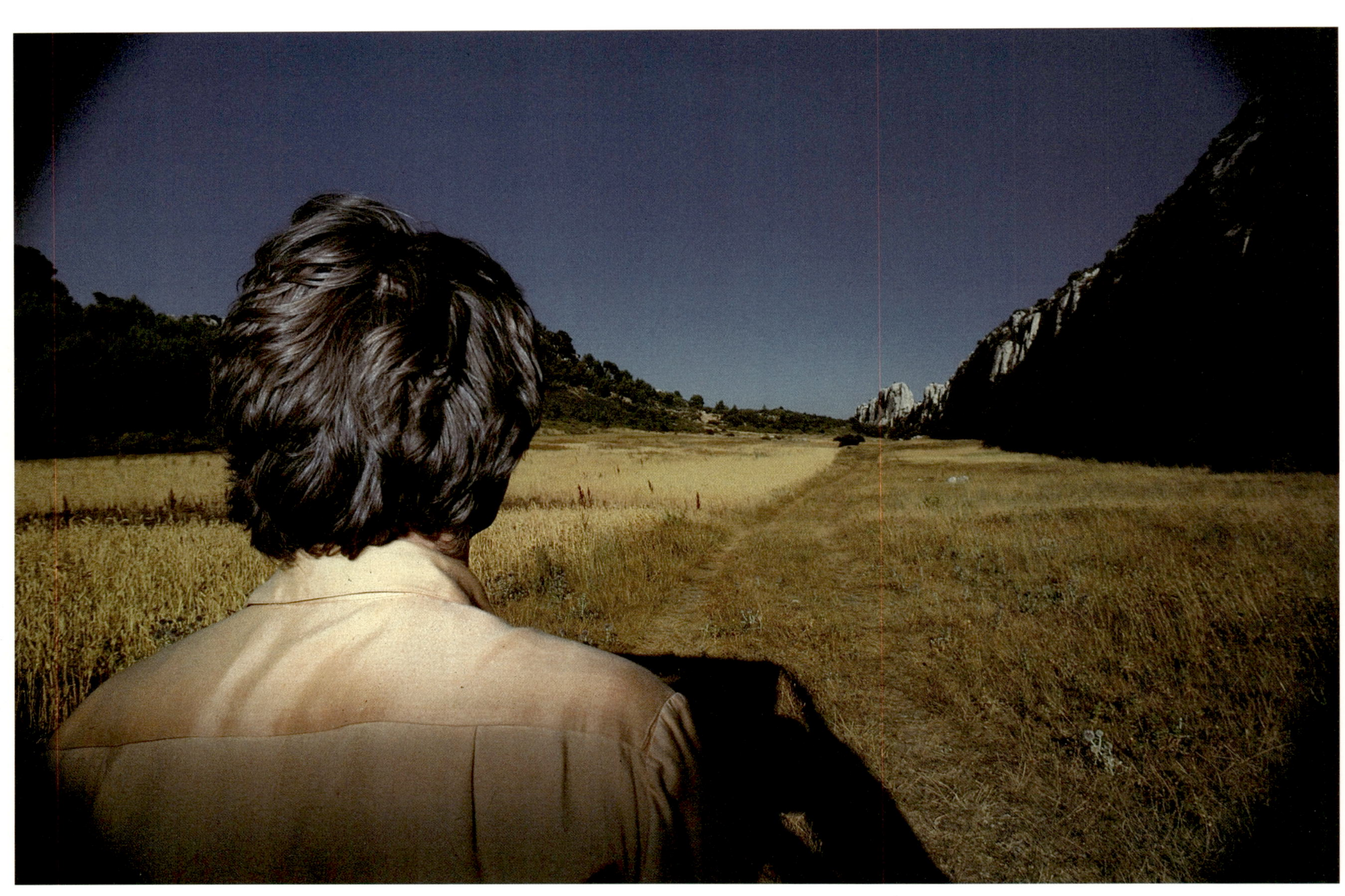

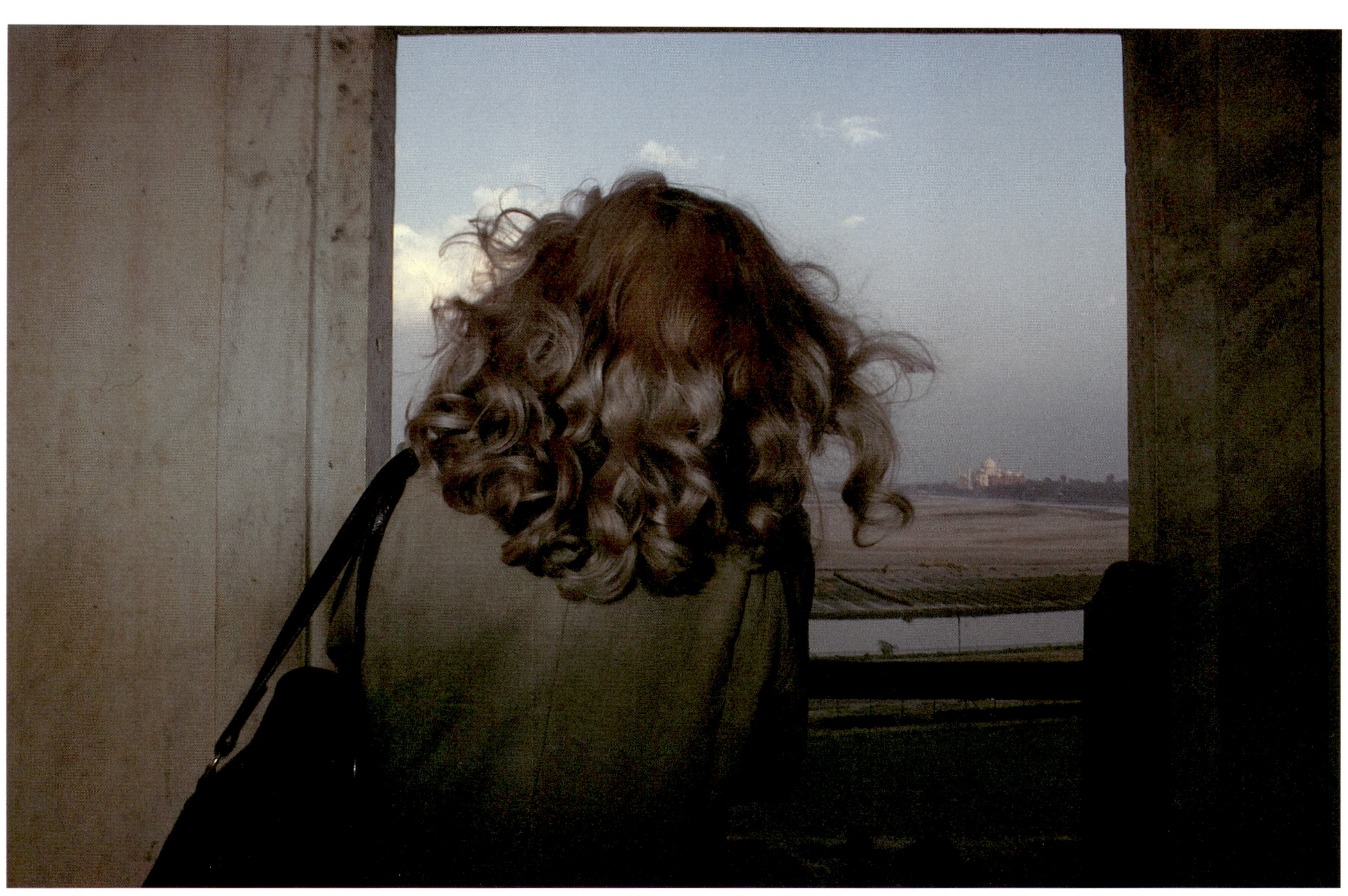

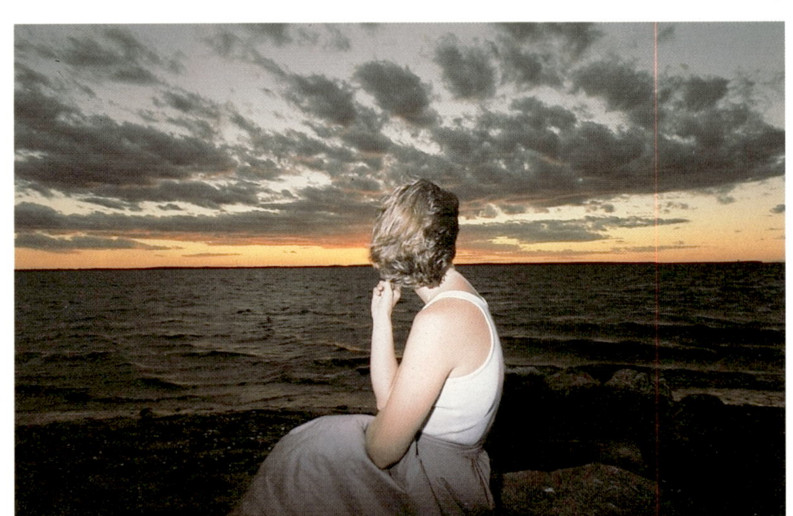